ORIGAMI
ARCHITECTURE

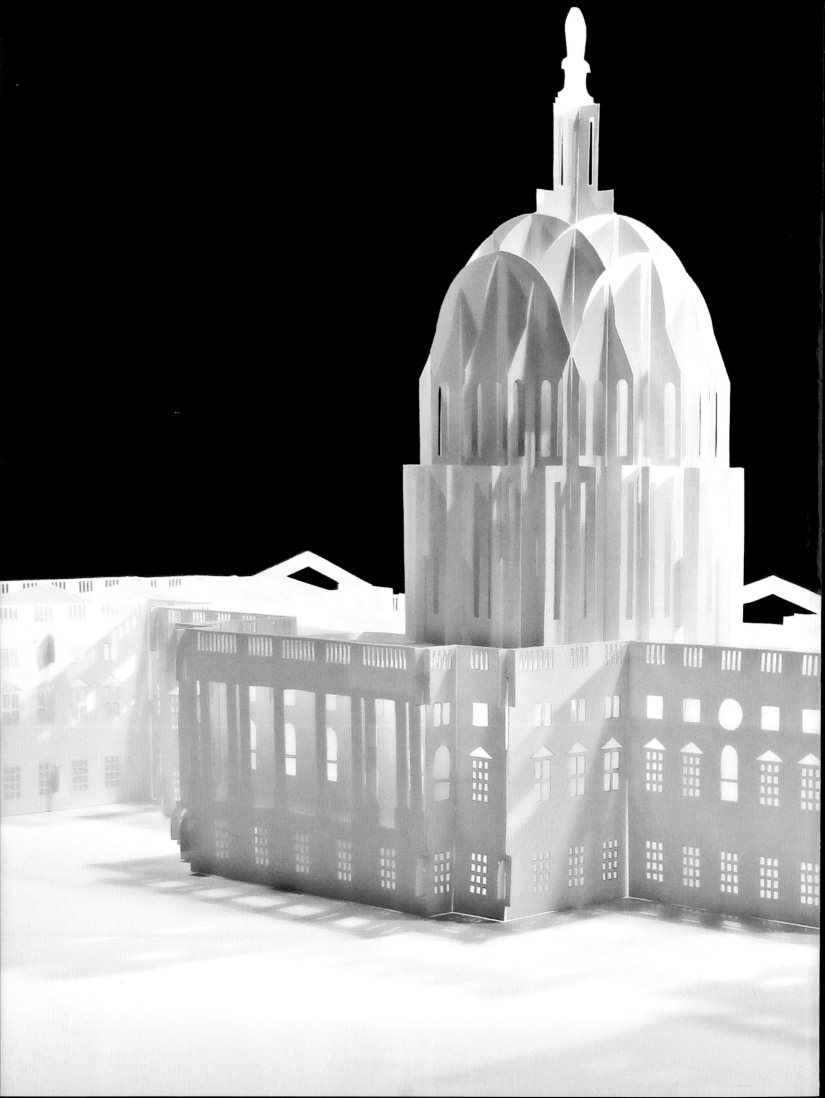

ORIGAMI
ARCHITECTURE
PAPERCRAFT MODELS OF THE WORLD'S MOST FAMOUS BUILDINGS

Yee

TUTTLE Publishing

Tokyo | Rutland, Vermont | Singapore

Published by Tuttle Publishing, an imprint of Periplus Editions (HK) Ltd.

www.tuttlepublishing.com

Library of Congress Cataloging-in-Publication Data

Yee, 1968-
 Origami architecture : papercraft models of the world's most famous
buildings / Yee.
    p. cm.

 ISBN 978-4-8053-1154-7 (pbk.)
 1. Origami. 2. Architectural models. 3. Cut-out craft. 4. Paper art. I. Title.
 TT870.Y427 2011
 736'.982--dc22

                    2011002818

 ISBN 978-4-8053-1154-7

Distributed by

North America, Latin America & Europe
Tuttle Publishing
364 Innovation Drive
North Clarendon, VT 05759-9436 U.S.A.
Tel: 1 (802) 773-8930
Fax: 1 (802) 773-6993
info@tuttlepublishing.com
www.tuttlepublishing.com

Japan
Tuttle Publishing
Yaekari Building, 3rd Floor
5-4-12 Osaki, Shinagawa-ku
Tokyo 141 0032
Tel: (81) 3 5437-0171
Fax: (81) 3 5437-0755
sales@tuttle.co.jp
www.tuttle.co.jp

First edition
16 15 14 13 12 11   1107EP
10 9 8 7 6 5 4 3 2 1

Printed in Hong Kong

TUTTLE PUBLISHING® is a registered trademark of
Tuttle Publishing, a division of Periplus Editions (HK) Ltd.

Table of Contents

INTRODUCTION

This book is filled with paper sculpture designs that will let you create paper replicas of some of the world's most beautiful and most famous buildings. The facade designs I've recreated are based on the real architecture of these buildings. Eight of sixteen buildings in this book use a uniquely designed interlocking system in which no glue is needed (except to glue the structure onto the baseboards). The other eight buildings are made with different folding mechanisms that need some glue to assemble them. I recommend using acid-free heavy paper for these projects, if you do, your building will last for many years and will resist turning brittle and yellow or fade with age. If you follow the provided instructions and cut each piece and assemble as directed, you'll see that making these sculptures is not really that difficult.

I'm particularly proud of the way these sculptures can be folded flat and opened again. This in itself is a fascinating part of the construct; if you tried to draw a diagram or analyze it, you would see the complexity that goes into this mechanism.

When the buildings are erected they are an amazing sight. I prefer to use white paper because the play of light and shade over a plain surface looks gorgeous, and more clearly reflects the structure of the piece. By contrast, a colored surface may be confusing because your eyes will focus on the two dimensional part of the structure and less on the three dimensional part of it. So leaving it plain and not coloring or decorating it is the best way to display your art work.

Although each of these structures is designed to fold, frequent opening and folding is not recommended due to the complexity and fragility of these paper structures. Keep it in an open position as much as you can and it will retain its beauty for years to come.

MY DESIGN PROCEDURE

1. After studying pictures of a building, I sketch a basic outline.

2. Then I use my computer to redraw the sketch.

3. Next, I design a feasible mechanism that makes the structure capable to stand and be folded.

4. I then select the artistic details of the structure that can be cut out of paper and add those.

5. Then I add other details to the drawings unless it might reduce the strength of the structure.

6. I go on to design a logical assembly procedure to make assembling easier.

7. Finally, I create a prototype. If it needs any adjustment, I go back and modify the drawings. I'll repeat this step again and again if necessary.

SUITABLE MATERIALS:

I use acid-free card stock, which can last for many years and will not turn brittle and yellow or fade with age. Card stock size is 8.5" x 11" (21.59 x 27.94 cm). Paperweight is between 60 lb to 120 lb (130 gsm to 260 gsm).

For the baseboards I recommend stiff cardboard of 220 lb (480 gsm) or more.

TOOLS:

1. **A sharp hobby knife:** the sharper the better. Either learn to sharpen the blades, or change blades whenever it begins to drag and catch.

2. **A burnishing tool:** This is handy for creasing a neat fold line. If you don't have a burnishing tool, an inkless ballpoint pen can work as well.

3. **A ruler:** It can be either a metal or plastic ruler. You can use it with a burnishing tool to crease a neat fold line.

4. **Cutting mat:** get the "self-healing" mats available in office and art supply stores. It is effective for protecting your table and your knife, more importantly, it makes cutting easier.

5. **Toothpicks:** For spreading glue.

6. **Tweezers:** For handling small parts.

7. **White glue:** This is perfect for gluing parts of the building because when it dries it's invisible and it holds paper very well. Be careful though, because once it's dried you won't be able to change anything without tearing the paper.

8. Ultimately, your head and hands are your most important tools—let them do as much of the work as possible.

GUIDELINES AND HINTS:

1. Please read through all the instructions for a building before you attempt to build it.

2. You must understand completely what you are trying to do before you do it.

3. Follow the step-by-step instructions as closely as you can.

4. Do not skip any steps, they are all important.

5   Always work on a flat, firm, and clean surface.

6   Crease with a burnishing tool and a ruler to make a neat fold line.

7   Be careful when you glue one piece to another. Once it dries there's no going back.

8   _____ Black solid lines on the templates represent cutting lines.

9   ------------------ Black dashed lines or _____ blue lines represents folding lines or gluing lines. The folding direction or gluing position is called out in the caption for the images.

10 Eight of sixteen buildings use an interlocking system, so no glue is applied (except gluing the building to the baseboards).

11 If you don't want the building to stick out from the baseboard when it is folded, you can increase the size of the baseboards.

12 Should your project not come out quite right or if you make a mistake, please don't give up. Remember that failure is always the best teacher.

TIPS FOR CUTTING

1   Always keep the blade sharp to reduce the need for pressure when cutting.

2   Keep your eyes on the cutting blade tip and cut slowly. With decent lighting and some practice anyone can make a nice clean cut.

3   Try to cut along the lines freehand. Don't rely on a steel ruler, over time steel rulers will sharpen and become dangerous to use.

4   Cut all the small shapes before cutting the big shapes.

5   If possible, cut the shape next to the shape you just cut.

6   Carefully use your fingers to press closely to the cutting area. But be careful.

BIOGRAPHY

My name is Yee (full name Sheung Yee Shing). I was born to a poor family in Hong Kong, where I didn't have toys as a child. Therefore, at a young age, I started to fold and cut old newspapers as a way to occupy myself. Later, I taught myself paper-cutting (silhouette) and started to design and handcraft toys with paper. Since then (around 36 years) I have been doing various papercrafts.

Creating and designing papercraft is both my hobby and job. Paper (one of the great inventions of Chinese) is one of the most interesting material, it has millions of possibilities. I am trying to discover as many of them as I can. I do paper-cutting, origami, pop up cards, origami architecture, paper toy, paper costume, paper lamp, and paper model, etc. Most of my designs and methods come entirely from my imagination. Once you have built a few of these buildings you will see why I love papercraft so much.

THE ARC DE TRIOMPHE
Paris, France

The Arc de Triomphe is the second largest triumphal arch in existence today. Emperor Napoleon I ordered the construction of the Arc de Triomphe to honor the Grande Armée that won the battle of Austerlitz in 1806. Designed by the French architect Jean Chalgrin, its design was mainly inspired by the Arch of Titus, a marble triumphal arch in Rome. The arch took thirty years to complete, long after Napoleon's death on St. Helena. It stands majestically at the center of the Place Charles de Gaulle, and from the roof of the arch are breathtaking views of Paris. Since its construction, many famous victory marches have gone by the shadow of the Arc de Triomphe, including the Germans in 1871, the French in 1918, the Germans again in 1940, and the French and Allied forces when Paris was liberated in 1944. Annually on July 14, Bastille Day (the French National Day), a military parade starts at the Arc de Triomphe and makes its way down the Champs Élysées.

The Arc de Triomphe is located in the center of the Place Charles de Gaulle, Paris. In terms of height, it stands tall at 162 feet or 49.5 meters. Its depth is measured at 72 feet or 22 meters, while its width is 150 feet or 45 meters.

Dimensions of the finished model:
(exclude baseboard)
7.77 inches or 19.7 cm in length
4.45 inches or 11.3 cm in width
8.07 inches or 20.5cm in height

Pieces count: 8 pieces (excluding the baseboard)

Difficulty level: 2/10 (easy)

Interlock pieces: Assemble the building without glue (excluding the baseboard).

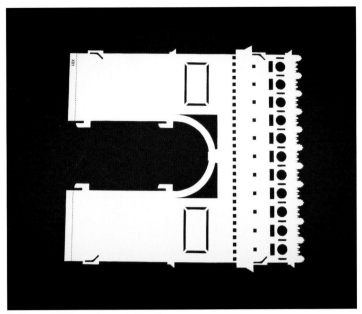

1. Cut out **X01** as shown in the figure.

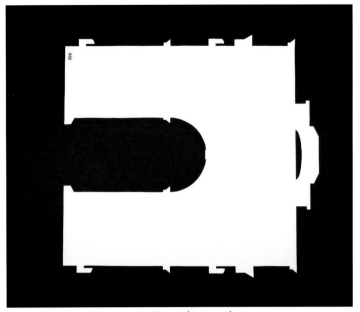

2. Cut out **X02** as shown in the figure. (2 pieces)

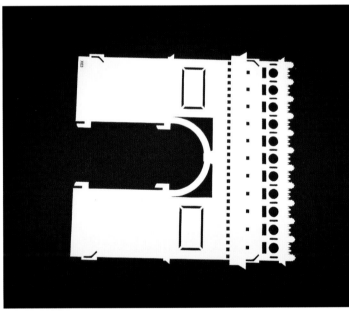

3. Cut out **X03** as shown in the figure.

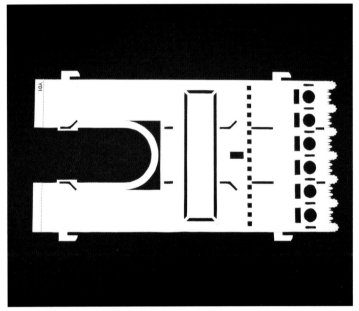

4. Cut out **Y01** as shown in the figure.

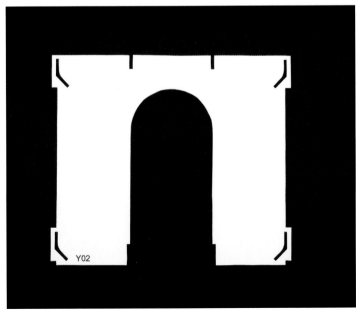

5. Cut out **Y02** as shown in the figure. (2 pieces)

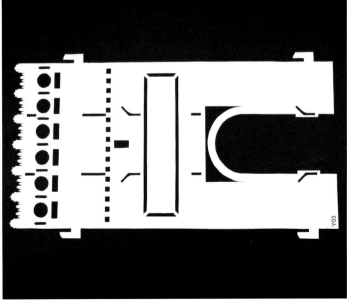

6. Cut out **Y03** as shown in the figure.

7. Fold the bottom parts of **X01** as shown in the figure.

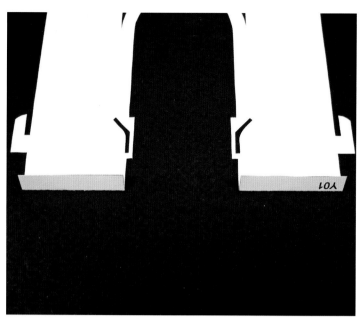

8. Fold the bottom parts of **Y01** as shown in the figure.

9. Interlock **X01** and **Y01** together as shown in the figure. Twist the tabs slightly while interlocking.

10. It should look like this after **X01** and **Y01** interlocked.

11. Interlock **X01** and **Y02** together as shown in the figure.

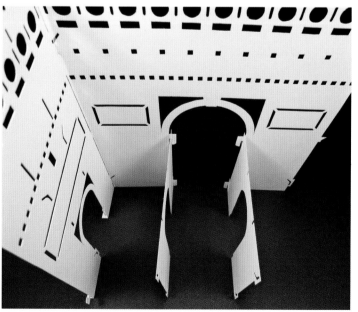

12. Interlock another **Y02** and **X01** together as shown in the figure.

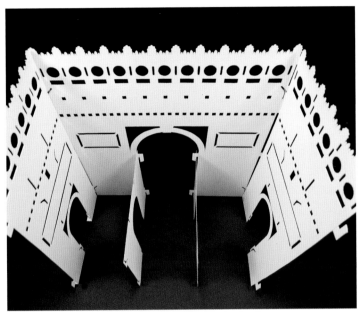

13. Interlock **X01** and **Y03** together as shown in the figure.

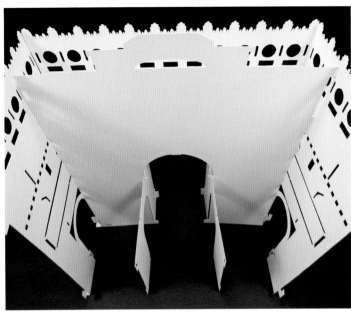

14. Interlock **X02** to **Y01** and **Y03** as shown in the figure.

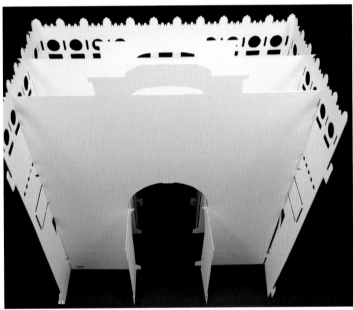

15. Interlock another **X02** to **Y01** and **Y03** as shown in the figure.

16. Interlock **X03** to **Y01**, **Y03** and two **Y02** as shown in the figure.

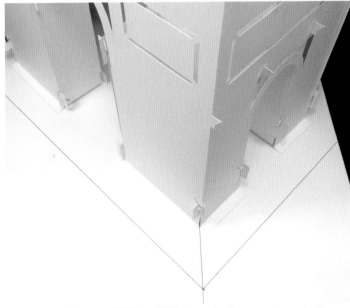

17. Glue folded parts of **X01** and **Y01** along the lines as shown in the figure.

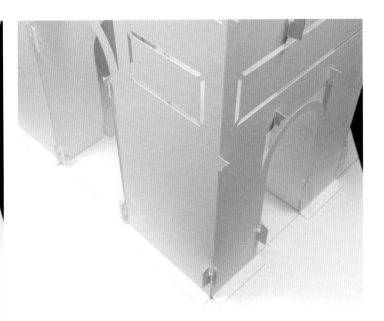

18. It should look like this after **X01** and **Y01** are glued. Erase remaining penciled lines.

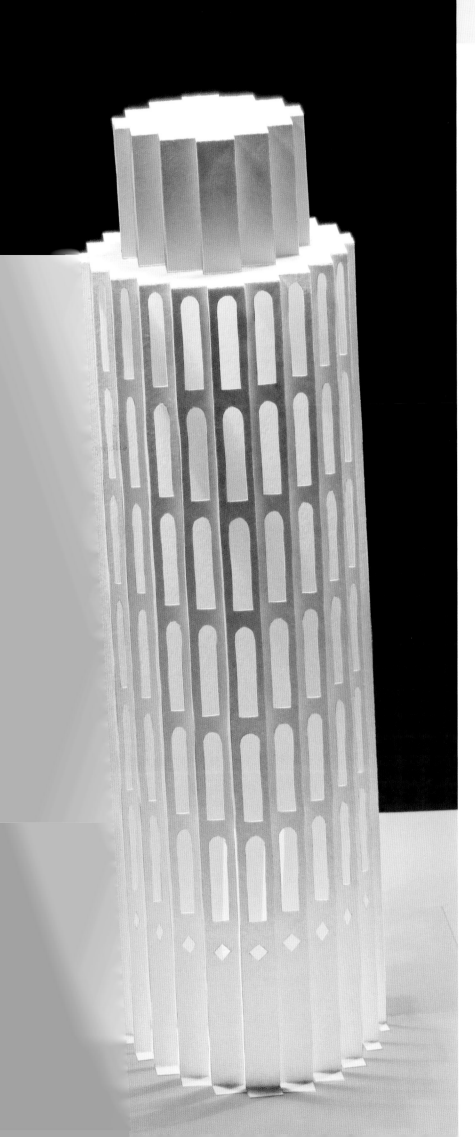

THE LEANING TOWER OF PISA
Pisa, Italy

The Leaning Tower of Pisa is the freestanding bell tower of the cathedral in the Italian city of Pisa. Construction of the tower began on August 8, 1173. Although unconfirmed, this Romanesque style tower may have been designed by Bonanno Pisano. The tower began to sink after construction had progressed to the third floor in 1178 and so construction was halted. In 1360, Tommaso Pisano completed the construction, erecting the belfry and making the last important geometric correction to the structure. In 1990 the tower was leaning 4/100 of inch (1 mm) every week. At this point it was generally thought that the tower would collapse unless something was done. Through the centuries, a number of projects have been implemented to stop the tower's lean. Finally a British engineering professor came up a solution to prevent the collapse by removing ground soil from under the high side of the tower. Work began in 1999 and it was completed at the beginning of June 2001. In May 2008, after the removal of 70 tons of earth, the tower had been stabilized. The engineers estimated that the tower would be stable for at least 200 years.

The Leaning Tower of Pisa stands at 183.3 feet or 55.8 meters from the ground on the low side and 186 feet or 56.7 meters on the high side.

Dimensions of the finished model:
(excluding the baseboard)
3.33 inches or 8.5 cm in length
2.74 inches or 7 cm in width
9.48 inches or 24 cm in height

Pieces count: 3 pieces (excluding the baseboard)

Difficulty level: 3/10 (easy)

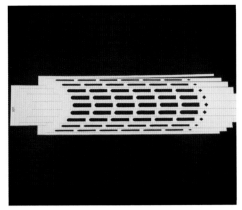

1. Cut out **X01** as shown in the figure.

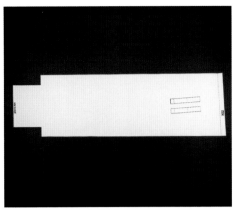

2. Cut out **X02** as shown in the figure.

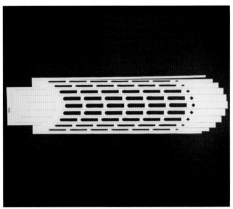

3. Cut out **X03** as shown in the figure.

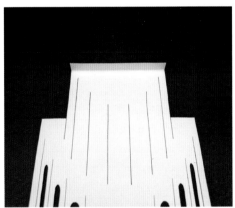

4. Flip **X01** over. Fold the upper part as shown in the figure.

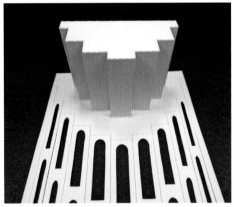

5. Fold these parts as shown in the figure.

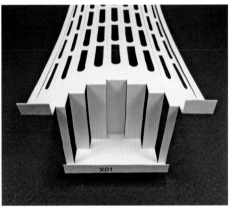

6. Fold these parts as shown in the figure.

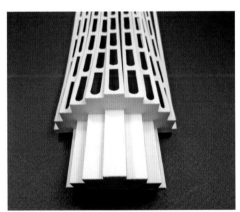

7. Fold these parts as shown in the figure.

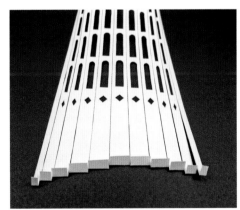

8. Fold these parts as shown in the figure.

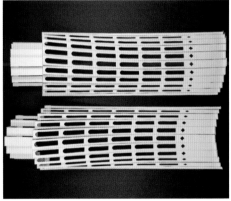

9. Repeat steps 4 to 8 to make two components.

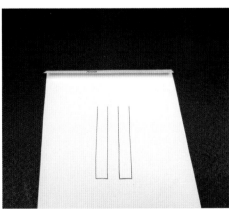

10. Flip **X02** over. Fold the bottom part as shown in the figure.

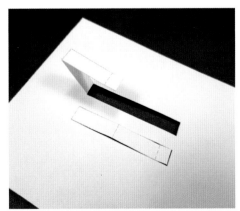

11. Fold this part as shown in the figure.

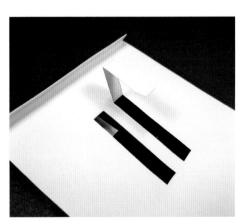

12. Fold this part as shown in the figure.

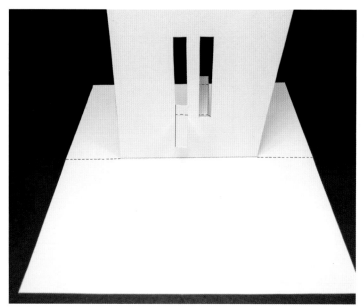

13. Glue the **X02** onto the baseboard as shown in the figure.

14. Glue **X01** onto **X02** as shown in the figure.

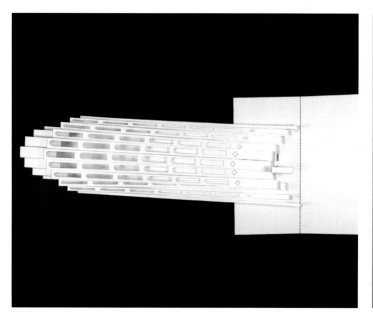

15. Fold down the building completely as shown in the figure.

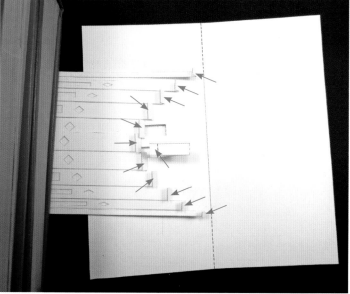

16. Use heavy books to weight the building. Apply glue as shown in the figure. Close the baseboard tightly. This will allow a perfect position for gluing.

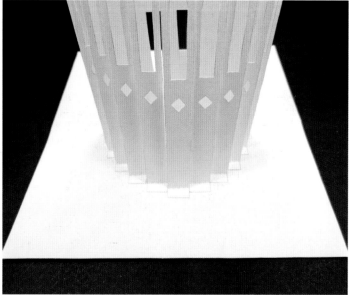

17. It should look like this after step 16 done.

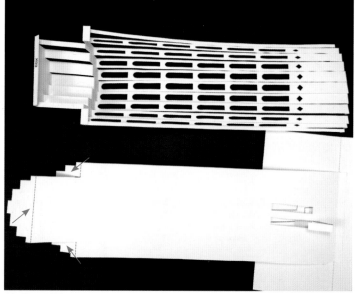

18. Glue **X03** onto **X02** as shown in the figure.

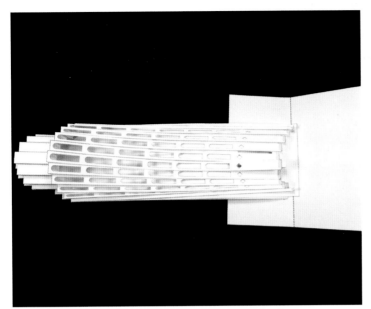

19. Fold down the building completely as shown in the figure.

20. Use heavy books to weight the building. Apply glue as shown in the figure. Close the baseboard tightly. They will find a perfect position to be glued.

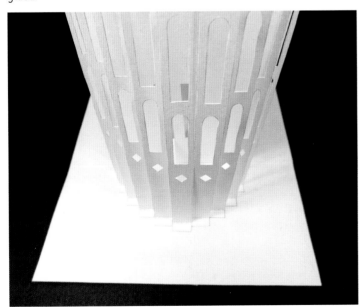

21. It should look like this after step 20 is done.

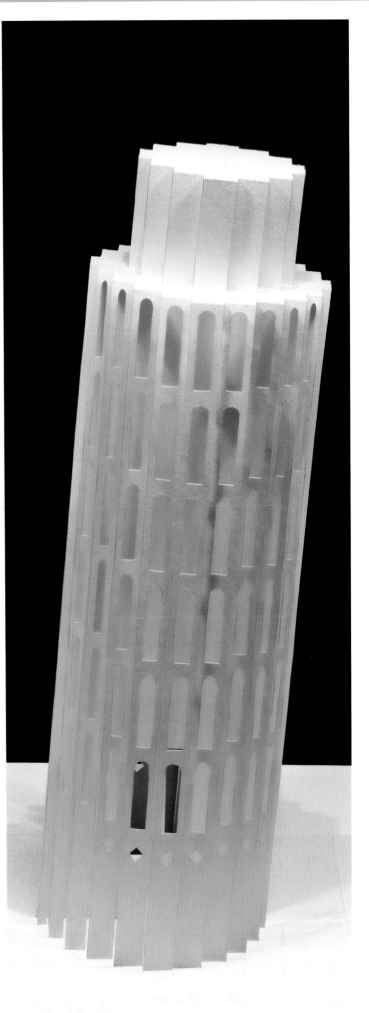

THE HALL OF SUPREME HARMONY
The Forbidden City, Beijing, China

W The Hall of Supreme Harmony is the largest hall found in within the Forbidden City in Beijing. It is first building you come to after passing through the Gate of Supreme Harmony. It is the largest wood building in China and one of the largest wood buildings in the world. It is the tallest building in the Forbidden City and is regarded as its most magnificent building. It was built during the Ming Dynasty in 1406 and was destroyed seven times by fires (mostly due to lightning strikes) during the Qing Dynasty and last re-built in 1695–1697. The interior is replete with dragons to signify the power of the nobility. It was built according to principles of Feng Shui with the numbers of five and nine being prominent in its building (auspicious numbers), including the Nine Dragon Screen and doors with nine rows of ornaments going up and down the pillars. The Last Emperor Puyi was crowned here in 1908 when he was three years old. Today over 7 million people visit the Forbidden City and its most famous structure each year.

The Hall of Supreme Harmony in terms of height, it stands tall at 88.3 feet or 26.92 meters. Its depth is measured at 157.5 feet or 48 meters, while its width is 311.7 feet or 95 meters.

Dimensions of the finished model:
(excluding the baseboard)
10.17 inches or 25.8 cm in length
5.91 inches or 15 cm in width
4.32 inches or 11 cm in height.

Pieces count: 17 pieces (excluding the baseboard)
Difficulty level: 3/10 (easy)

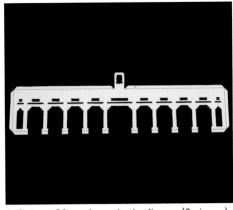

1. Cut out **C1** as shown in the figure. (2 pieces)

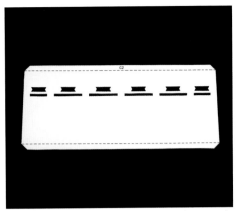

2. Cut out **C2** as shown in the figure. (2 pieces)

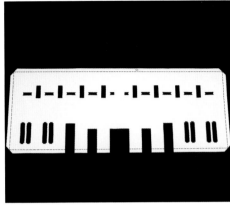

3. Cut out **C3** as shown in the figure. (2 pieces)

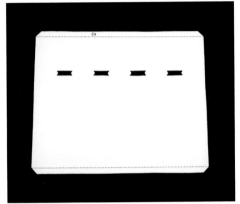

4. Cut out **C4** as shown in the figure. (2 pieces)

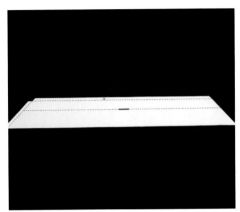

5. Cut out **C5** as shown in the figure. (2 pieces)

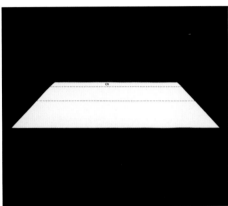

6. Cut out **C6** as shown in the figure. (2 pieces)

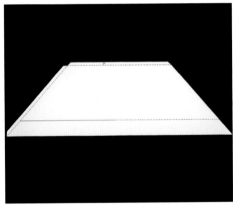

7. Cut out **C7** as shown in the figure. (2 pieces)

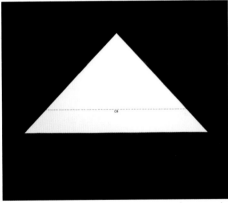

8. Cut out **C8** as shown in the figure. (2 pieces)

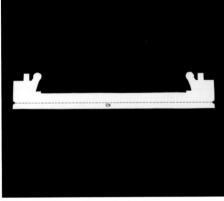

9. Cut out **C9** as shown in the figure.

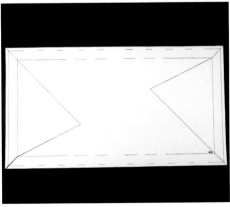

10. Cut out **C10** as shown in the figure

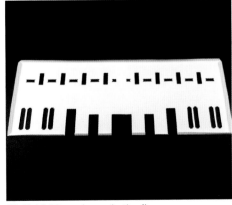

11. Fold **C3** as shown in the figure.

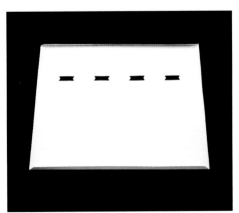

12. Fold **C4** as shown in the figure.

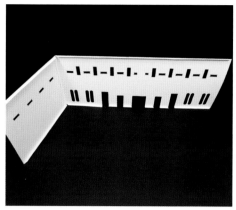

13. Apply glue on the folded edge to join **C3** and **C4** together as shown in the figure.

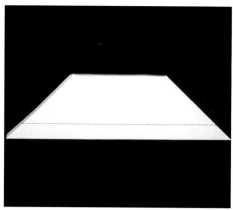

14. Fold **C7** as shown in the figure.

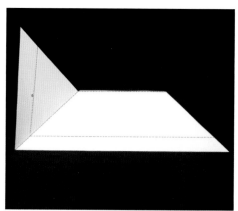

15. Apply glue on the folded edge to join **C7** and **C8** together as shown in the figure.

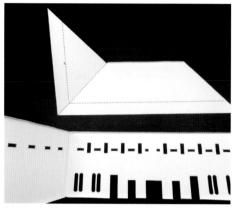

16. Apply glue on the folded edge to join two units together as shown in the figure.

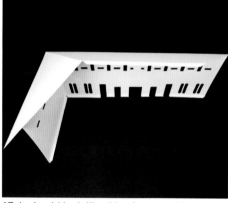

17. It should look like this after step 16 done.

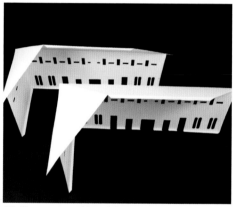

18. Repeat step 11 to 16 to make two components total.

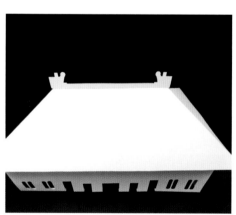

19. Glue **C9** on one of the component from step 18 as shown in the figure.

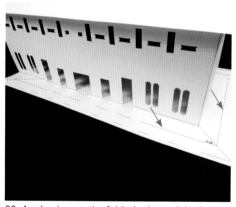

20. Apply glue on the folded edge to join the baseboard as shown in the figure.

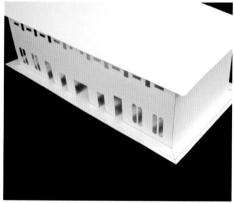

21. It should look like this after step 20 done.

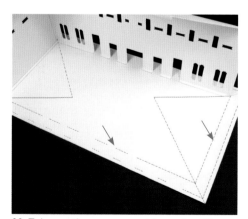

22. Take another component from step 18. Apply glue on the folded edge to join the baseboard as shown in the figure.

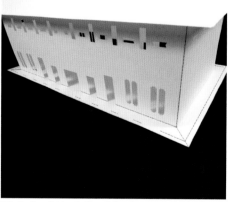

23. It should look like this after step 22 is done.

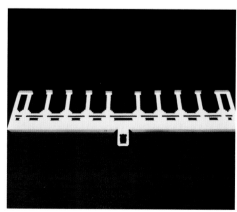

24. Fold **C1** as shown in the figure.

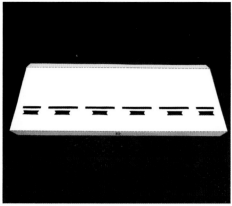

25. Fold **C2** as shown in the figure.

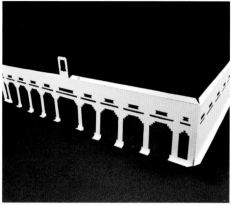

26. Apply glue on the folded edge to join two pieces together as shown in the figure.

27. Fold **C5** as shown in the figure.

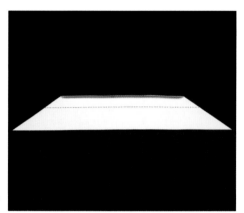

28. Fold **C6** as shown in the figure.

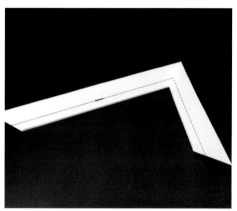

29. Apply glue on the folded edge to join the two pieces together as shown in the figure.

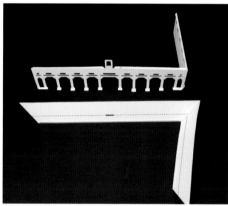

30. Apply glue on the folded edge to join two pieces together as shown in the figure.

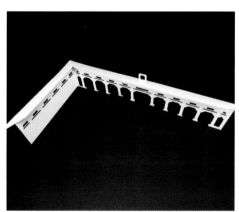

31. It should look like this after step 30 is done.

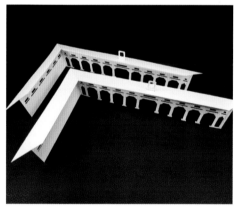

32. Repeat step 24 to 30 to make two components.

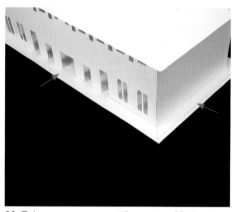

33. Take one component from step 32. Apply glue on the folded edge to join baseboard as shown in the figure.

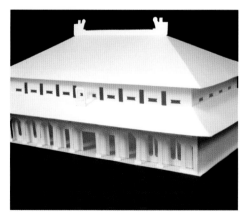

34. It should look like this after step 33 done.

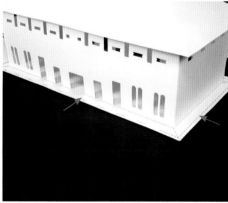

35. Take another component from step 32. Apply glue on the folded edge to join the baseboard as shown in the figure

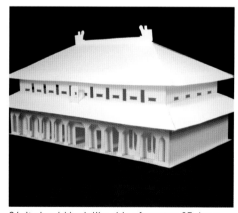

36. It should look like this after step 35 done.

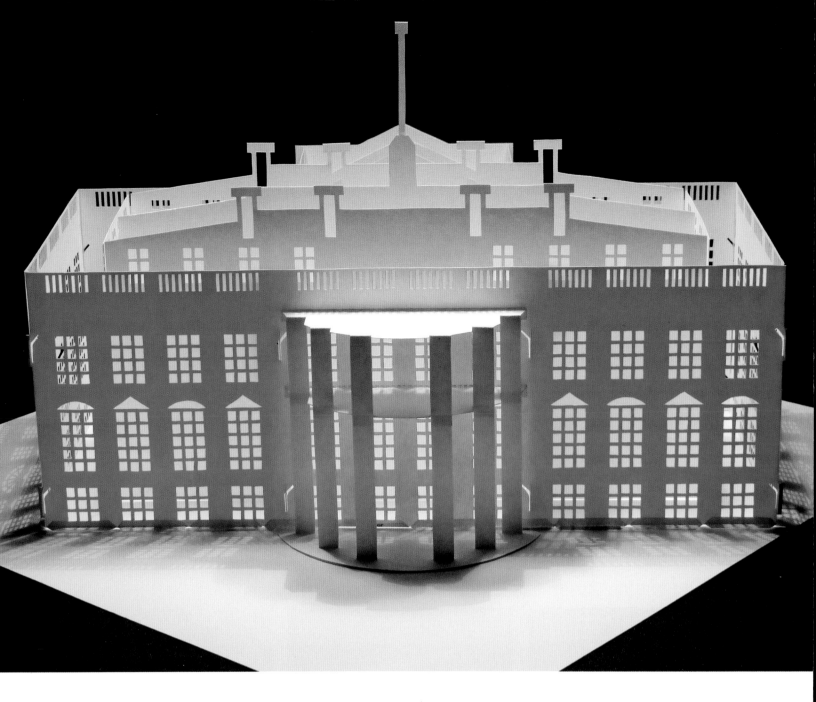

THE WHITE HOUSE
Washington D.C., USA

The White House is the main workplace and official home of the President of the United States. It has been the residence of every U.S. President since John Adams took up residency in 1800. The building is done in neoclassical stye and is made of Aquia stone, and painted white. The construction began in October 1792 and the building was completed in 1800. In 1814 the White House was set on fire by the British during the War of 1812. It was rebuilt after the fire and continued to undergo minor changes by subsequent presidents. The Truman administration was forced to close down the building because it was starting to show signs of serious wear and stress. A complete renovation went underway, rebuilding the superstructure using steel instead of timber. The Kennedys redecorated many of the rooms during their administration, giving it the elegant look it has today. The White House is an accredited museum with over 5000 people visiting each day.

The White House is in Washington, DC. It stands 70 feet or 21.3 meters in height. Its depth is 152 feet or 46.3 meters, while its width is 168 feet or 51.2 meters.

Dimensions of the finished model:
(excluding the baseboard)
10.31 inches or 26.2 cm in length
8.94 inches or 22.7 cm in width
6.41 inches or 16.3 cm in height.

Pieces count: 32 pieces (excluding the baseboard)

Difficulty level: 3/10 (easy)

Interlock pieces: Assemble the building without glue (excluding the baseboard).

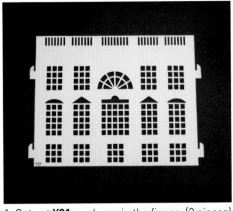

1. Cut out **Y01** as shown in the figure. (2 pieces)

2. Cut out **Y02** as shown in the figure. (2 pieces)

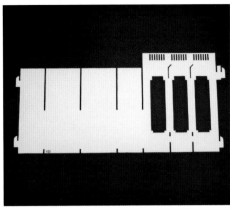

3. Cut out **Y03** as shown in the figure. (2 pieces)

4. Cut out **X01** as shown in the figure.

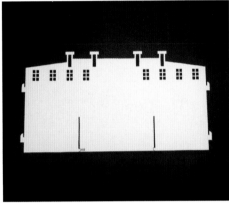

5. Cut out **X02** as shown in the figure. (2 pieces)

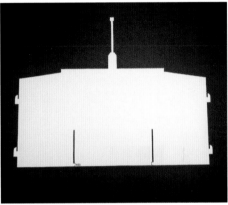

6. Cut out **X03** as shown in the figure.

7. Cut out **X04** as shown in the figure.

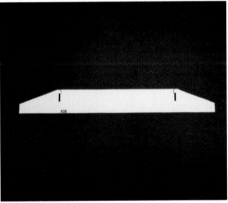

8. Cut out **X05** as shown in the figure.

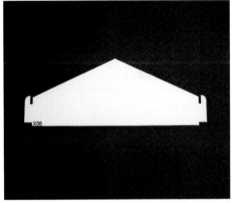

9. Cut out **X06** as shown in the figure. (2 pieces)

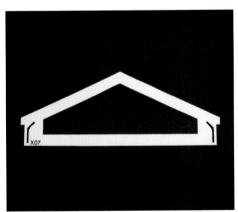

10. Cut out **X07** as shown in the figure.

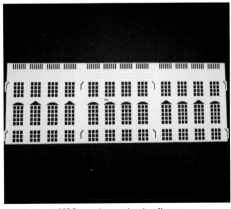

11. Cut out **X08** as shown in the figure.

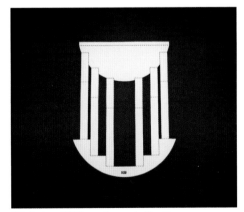

12. Cut out **X09** as shown in the figure.

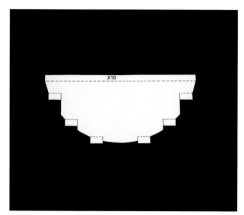

13. Cut out **X10** as shown in the figure.

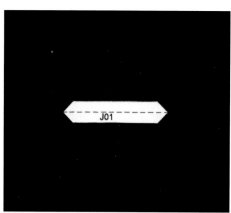

14. Cut out **J01** as shown in the figure. (14 pieces)

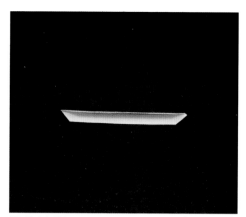

15. Fold **J01** as shown in the figure. (14 pieces)

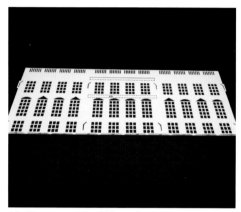

16. Glue ten of the **J01** on the bottom of **X08** as shown in the figure.

17. Glue four of the **J01** on the bottom of **Y01** as shown in the figure.

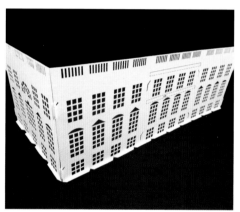

18. Interlock **Y01** and **X08** together as shown in the figure.

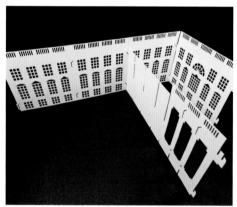

19. Interlock **Y03** and **X08** together as shown in the figure.

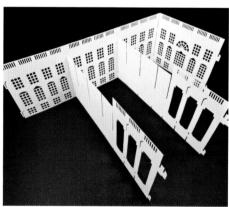

20. Interlock another **Y03** to **X08** as shown in the figure.

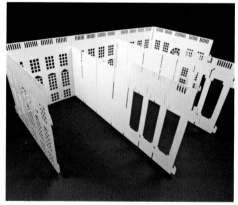

21. Interlock another **Y01** to **X08** as shown in the figure.

22. Interlock **X02** to the slots as shown in the figure.

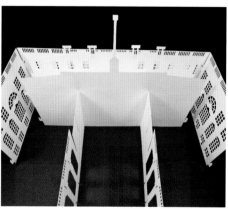

23. Interlock **X03** to the slots as shown in the figure.

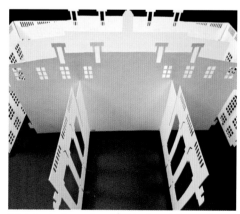

24. Interlock another **X02** to the slots as shown in the figure.

25. Interlock **Y02** as shown in the figure.

26. Interlock **Y02** on the other side as shown in the figure.

27. Interlock **X01** as shown in the figure.

28. Interlock **X05** as shown in the figure.

29. Interlock another **X05** as shown in the figure.

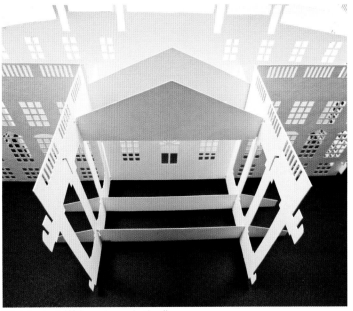
30. Interlock **X06** as shown in the figure.

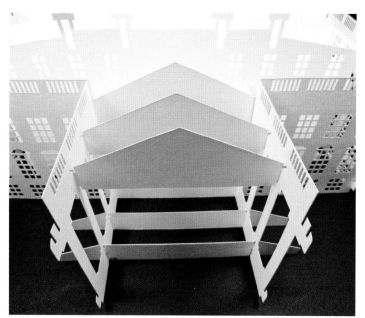

31. Interlock another **X06** as shown in the figure.

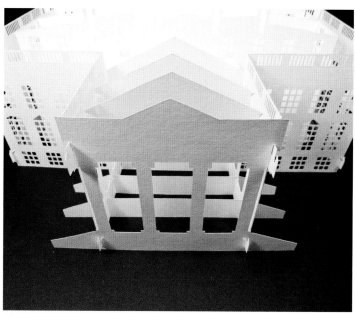

32. Interlock **X04** as shown in the figure.

33. Interlock **X07** as shown in the figure.

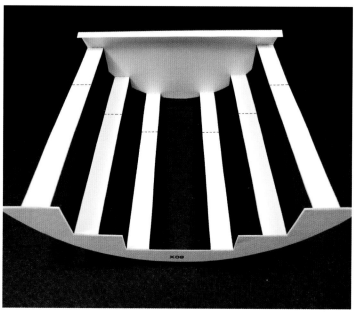

34. Fold **X09** as shown in the figure.

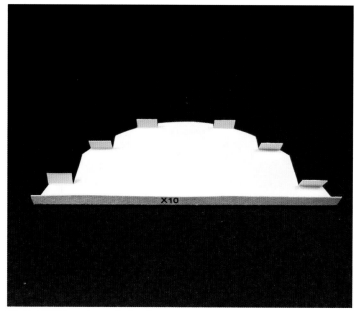

35. Fold **X10** as shown in the figure.

36. Apply glue to join **X09** and **X10** together as shown in the figure.

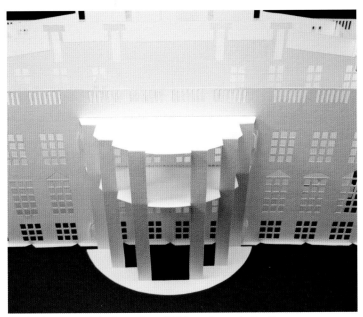

37. Apply glue to join the unit and **X08** as shown in the figure.

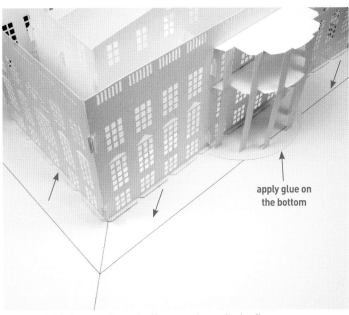

apply glue on
the bottom

38. Glue folded parts along the lines as shown in the figure.

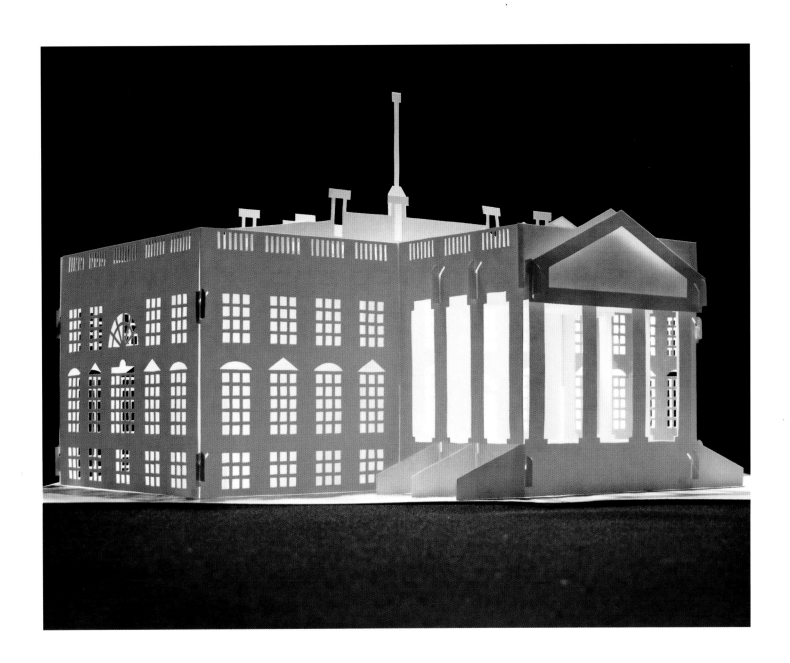

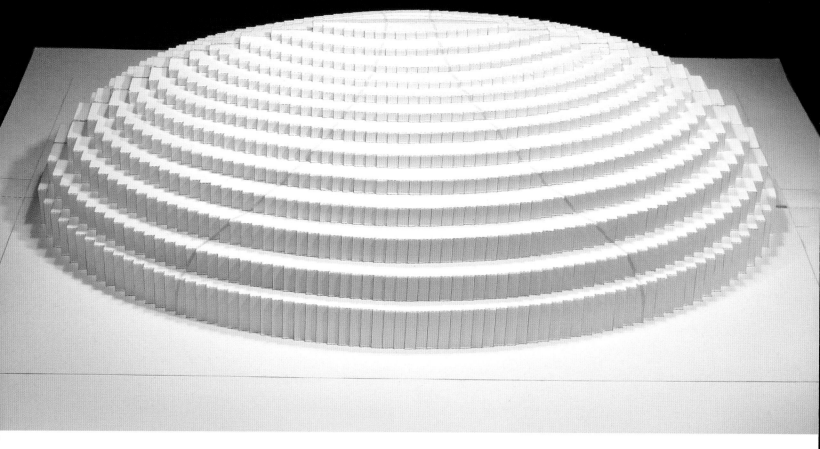

THE NATIONAL CENTER FOR THE PERFORMING ARTS
Beijing, China

The National Center for the Performing Arts is formally known as the National Grand Theatre is in Beijing, People's Republic of China. This controversial building was designed by French architect Paul Andreu, and construction started in December 2001. In July 2007, the construction was completed and the inaugural concert was held in December 2007. Surrounded by an artificial lake, it looks like an egg floating on reflective waters. Part of China's campaign to create a more vibrant and contemporary image of China, the center is an ellipsoid dome of titanium and glass that seats 5,452 people in its three halls. Opera is extremely popular and well attended in China, but the building also hosts concerts, plays, and other live arts events. The Center's location is immediately to the west of Tiananmen Square and the Great Hall of the People, and near the Forbidden City.

The National Center for the Performing Arts China
in terms of height, it stands tall at 151 feet or 46 meters. Its depth is measured at 472.4 feet or 144 meters, while its width is 695.5 feet or 212 meters.

Dimensions of the finished model:
(excluding the baseboard)
9.58 inches or 24.3 cm in length
6.64 inches or 16.8 cm in width
2.55 inches or 6.5 cm in height.

Pieces count: 3 pieces (excluding baseboard)

Difficulty level: 4/10 (easy)

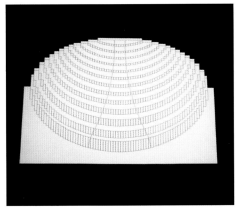

1. Cut it out from page 01 as shown in the figure. Cut all the solid lines. Score the entire crease (dashed line).

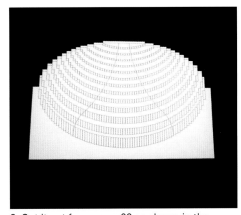

2. Cut it out from page 02 as shown in the figure. Cut all the solid lines. Score the entire crease (dashed line)

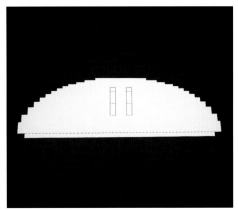

3. Cut it out from page 03 as shown in the figure. Cut all the solid lines. Score the entire crease (dashed line)

4. Lift and push out the first level structure gently as shown in the figure.

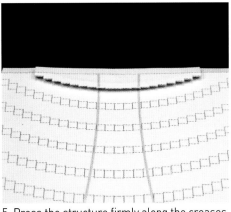

5. Press the structure firmly along the creases to make the fold complete as shown in the figure.

6. Lift and push out the second level structure gently as shown in the figure.

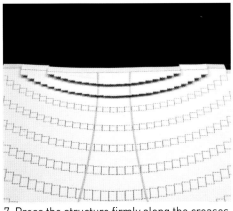

7. Press the structure firmly along the creases to make the fold complete as shown in the figure.

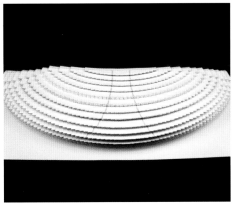

8. Keep repeating this procedure folding all levels completely as shown in the figure.

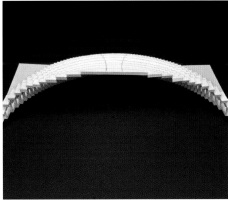

9. Fold down the base level as shown in the figure.

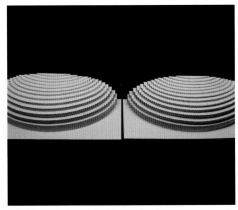

10. Repeat step 4 to 9 to make two components as shown in the figure.

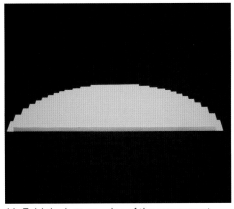

11. Fold the bottom edge of the component from step 3 as shown in the figure.

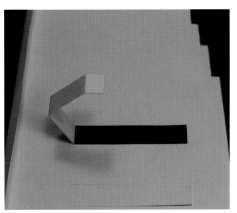

12. Fold the piece as shown in the figure.

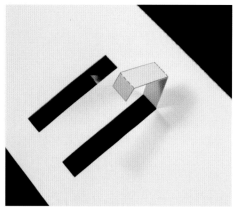

13. Flip over. Fold the other piece as shown in the figure.

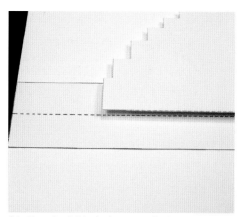

14. Glue the folded edge onto the baseboard as shown in the figure.

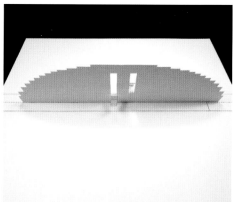

15. It should look like this after step 14 done.

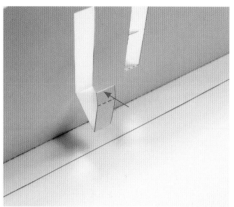

16. Apply glue as shown in the figure. Close the baseboard tightly. It will find a perfect position to be cohered.

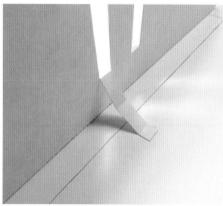

17. It should look like this after step 16 done.

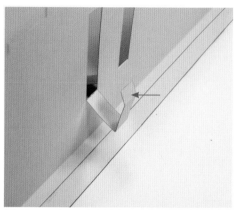

18. Rotate the unit 180 degrees. Apply glue as shown in the figure. Close the baseboard tightly. It will find a perfect position to be cohered.

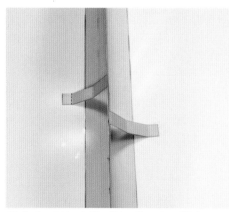

19. It should look like this after step 18 done.

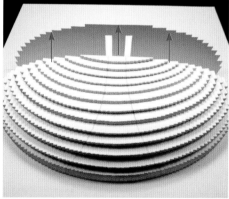

20. Take one component in step 10. Apply glue on the gluing edges as shown in the figure.

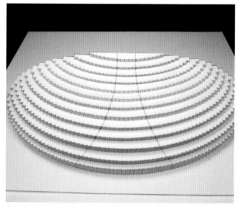

21. It should look like this after the two components are together.

22. Take another component in step 10. Apply glue to the edges to cohere as shown in the figure.

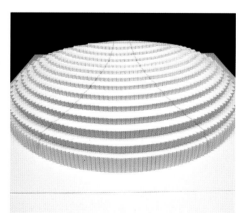

23 It should look like this after the two components are glued together.

24. Apply glue to the underbelly to cohere as shown in the figure.

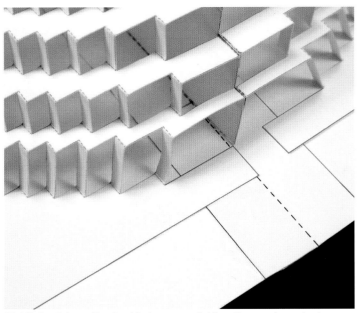

25. While gluing, align it with the center folding line as shown in the figure.

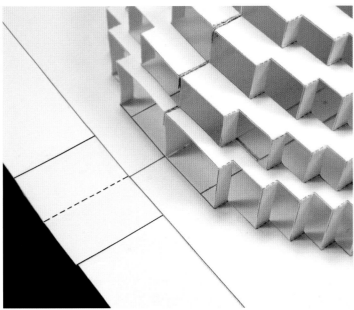

26. While gluing, align it with the center folding line as shown in the figure.

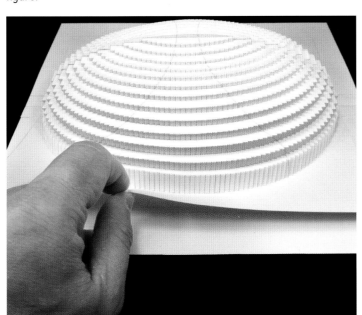

27. Rotate the unit 180 degrees. Apply glue to the underbelly to cohere as shown in the figure.

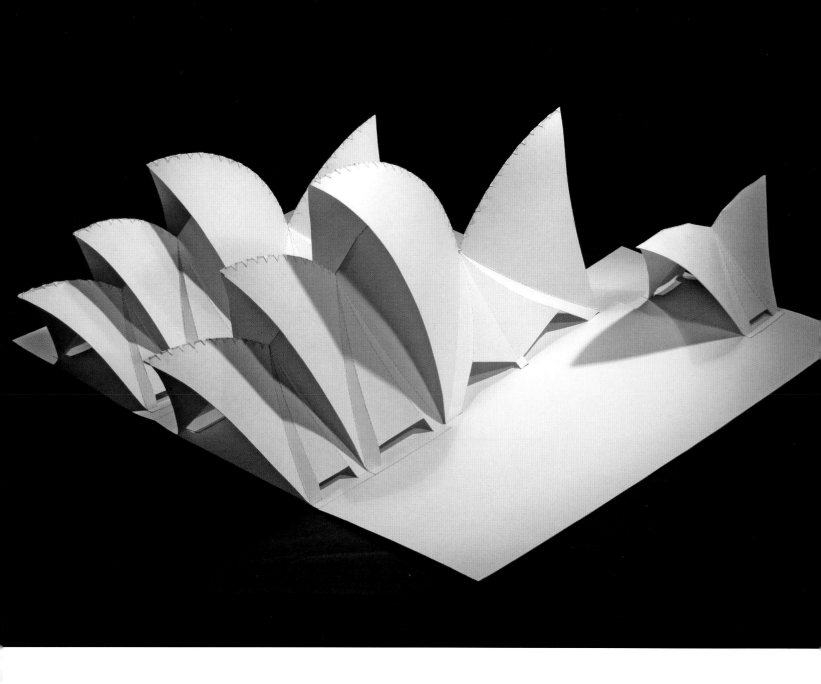

SYDNEY OPERA HOUSE
Sydney, Australia

The creative and stunning design by Danish architect Jørn Utzon (who in 2003 received the Pritzker Prize, architecture's highest honor) with enormous shell-like roofs was well ahead of its time. Controversy surrounded the building as the project was completed ten years later than anticipated and more than fourteen times over its original budget. No one doubts today its value for Australia as an iconic landmark and a representation of a whole country. It houses both a symphony hall and an opera hall, and is listed has a UNESCO World Heritage site. It is located on Bennelong Point in Sydney Harbour, close to the Sydney Harbour Bridge. It sits at the northeastern tip of the Sydney central business district, surrounded on three sides by the harbor (Sydney Cove and Farm Cove) and neighbored by the Royal Botanic Gardens.

Dimensions of the finished model:
(including baseboard)
11.61 inches or 29.5 cm in length
10.23 inches or 26 cm in width
4.72 inches or 12 cm in height.

Pieces count: 16 pieces (including baseboard)

Difficulty level: 4/10 (easy)

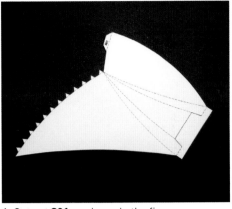

1. Cut out **S01** as shown in the figure.

2. Cut out **S02** as shown in the figure.

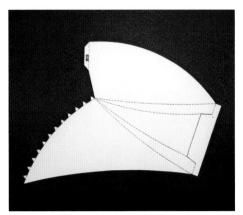

3. Cut out **S03** as shown in the figure.

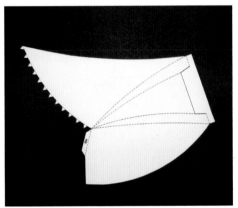

4. Cut out **S04** as shown in the figure.

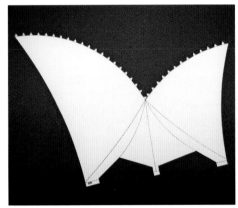

5. Cut out **S05** as shown in the figure.

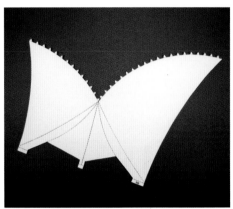

6. Cut out **S06** as shown in the figure.

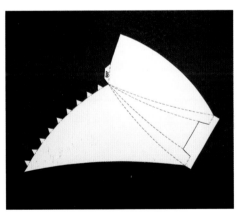

7. Cut out **S07** as shown in the figure.

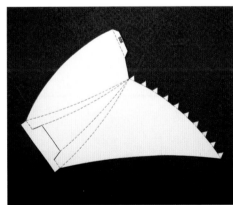

8. Cut out **S08** as shown in the figure.

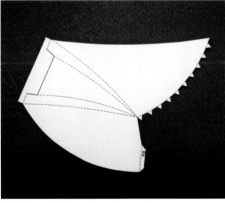

9. Cut out **S09** as shown in the figure.

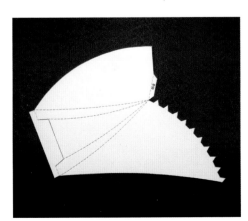

10. Cut out **S10** as shown in the figure.

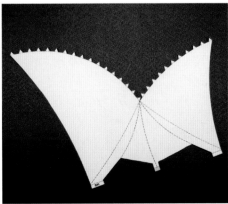

11. Cut out **S11** as shown in the figure.

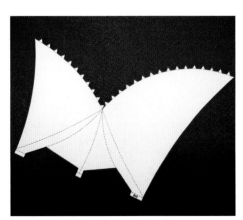

12. Cut out **S12** as shown in the figure.

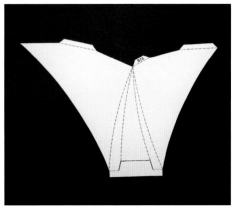

13. Cut out **S13** as shown in the figure.

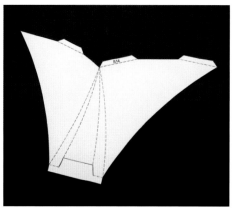

14. Cut out **S14** as shown in the figure.

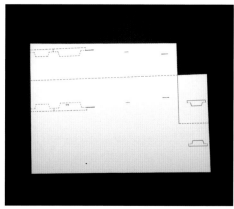

15. Cut out **S15** as shown in the figure.

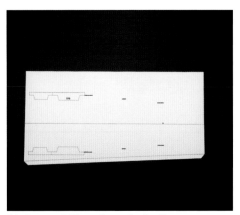

16. Cut out **S16** as shown in the figure.

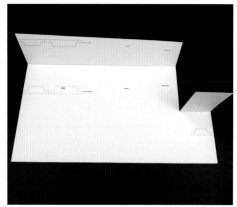

17. Fold **S15** as shown in the figure.

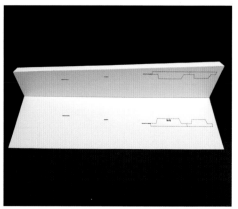

18. Fold **S16** as shown in the figure.

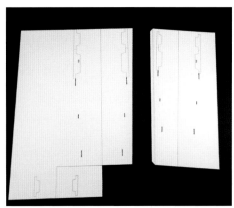

19. Use glue on the folded edge and cohere as shown in the figure.

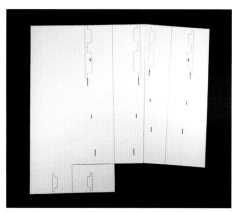

20. It should look like this after step 19 done.

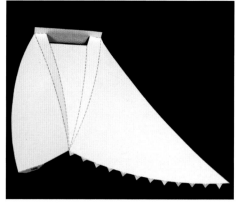

21. Fold **S01** as shown in the figure.

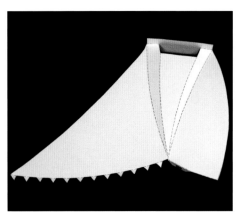

22. Fold **S02** as shown in the figure.

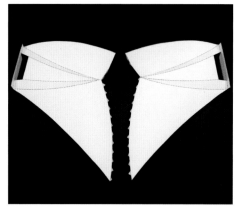

23. Apply glue to join **S01** and **S02** as shown in the figure.

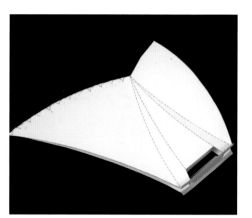

24. It should look like this after **S01** and **S02** joined.

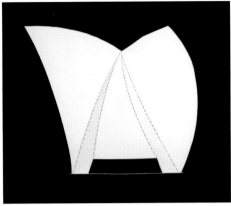

25. Fold **S03** as shown in the figure.

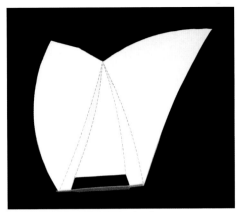

26. Fold **S04** as shown in the figure.

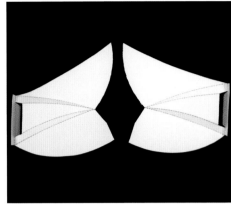

27. Apply glue to join **S03** and **S04** as shown in the figure.

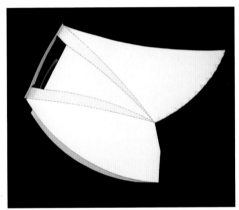

28. It should look like this after **S03** and **S04** joined.

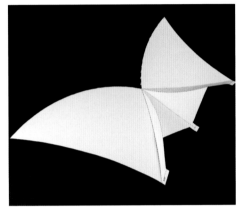

29. Fold **S05** as shown in the figure.

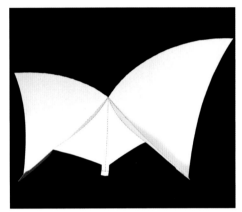

30. Fold **S06** as shown in the figure.

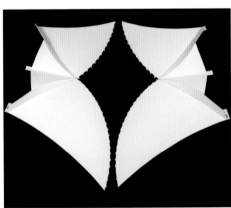

31. Apply glue to join **S05** and **S06** as shown in the figure.

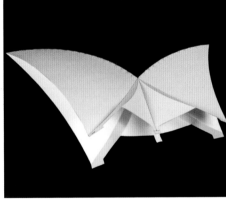

32. It should look like this after **S05** and **S06** joined.

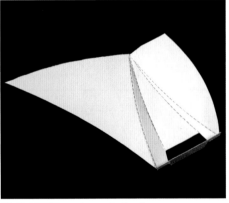

33. Fold **S07** as shown in the figure.

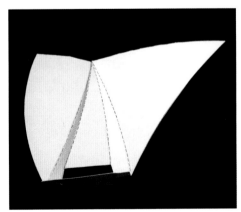

34. Fold **S08** as shown in the figure.

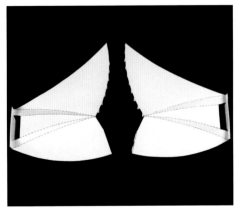

35. Apply glue to join **S07** and **S08** as shown in the figure.

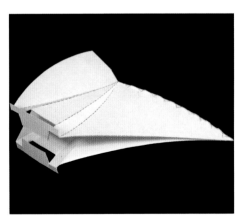

36. It should look like this after **S07** and **S08** joined.

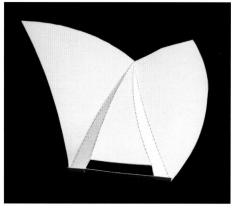

37. Fold **S09** as shown in the figure.

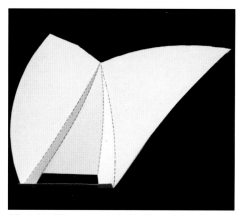

38. Fold **S10** as shown in the figure.

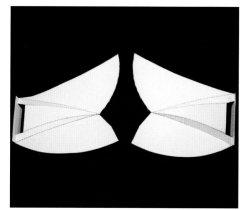

39. Apply glue to join **S09** and **S10** as shown in the figure.

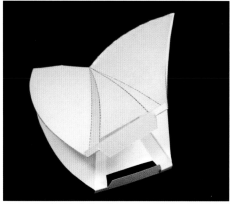

40. It should look like this after **S09** and **S10** joined.

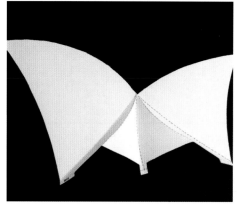

41. Fold **S11** as shown in the figure.

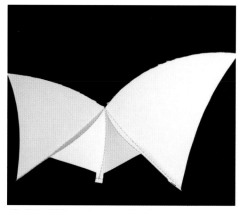

42. Fold **S12** as shown in the figure.

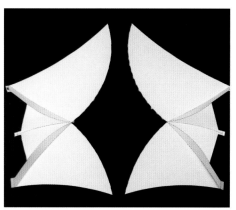

43. Apply glue to join **S11** and **S12** as shown in the figure.

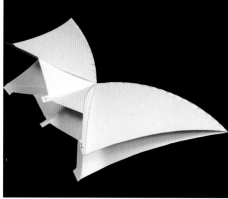

44. It should look like this after **S11** and **S12** joined.

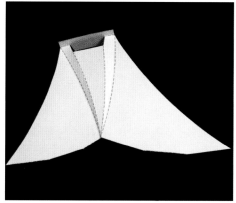

45. Fold **S13** as shown in the figure.

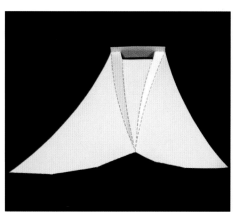

46. Fold **S14** as shown in the figure.

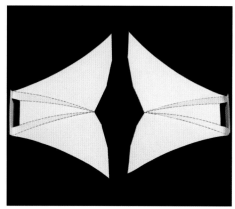

47. Apply glue to join **S13** and **S14** as shown in the figure.

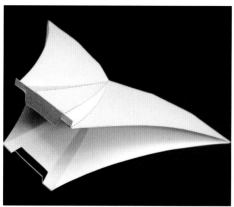

48. It should look like this after **S13** and **S14** joined.

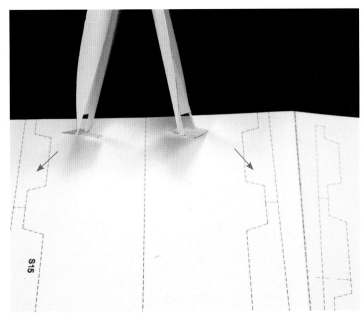

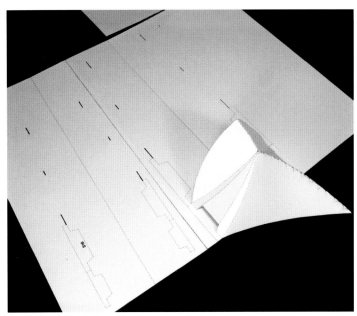

49. Take the unit in step 24. Glue it on the baseboard as shown in the figure.

50. It should look like this after step 49 done.

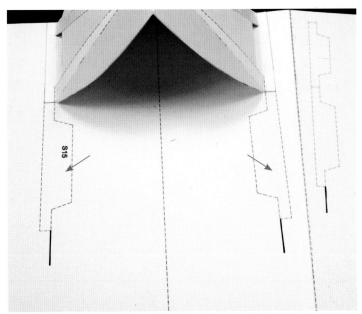

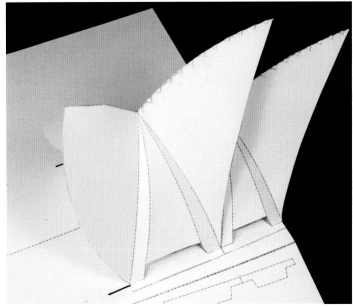

51. Take the unit in step 24. Glue it on the baseboard as shown in the figure.

52. It should look like this after step 51 done.

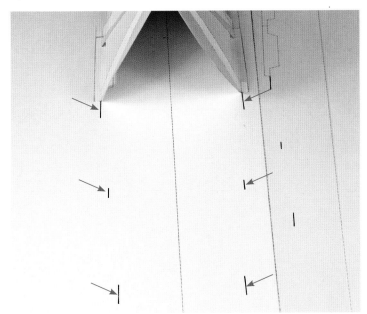

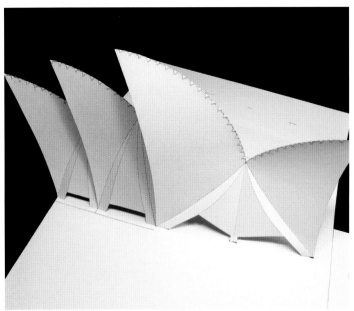

53. Take the unit in step 32. Tuck those legs through the slots on the baseboard. Fold and glue them to the underbelly as shown in the figure.

54. It should look like this after step 53 done.

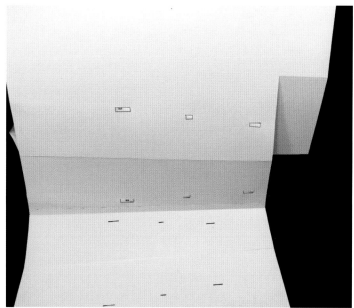

55. It should look like this underneath.

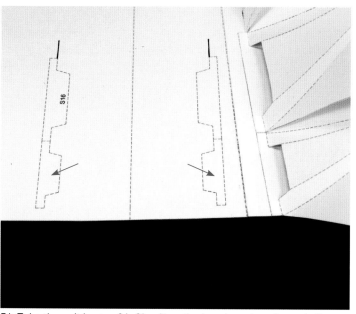

56. Take the unit in step 36. Glue it on the baseboard as shown in the figure.

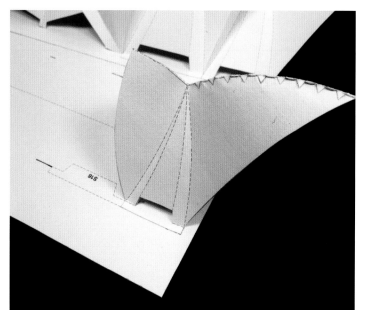

57. It should look like this after step 56 done.

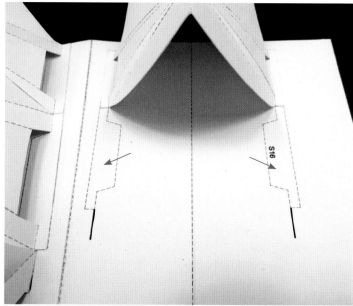

58. Take the unit in step 40. Glue it on the baseboard as shown in the figure.

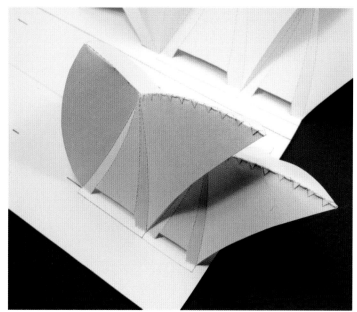

59. It should look like this after step 58 done.

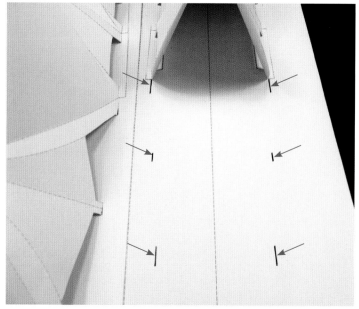

60. Take the unit in step 44 and glue it on the baseboard as shown in the figure..

61. Tuck those legs through the slots on the baseboard. Fold and glue them to the underbelly as shown in the figure.

62. It should look like this underbelly after step 61 done.

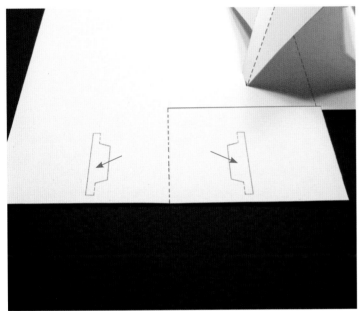

63. Take the unit in step 48 and glue it on the baseboard as shown above.

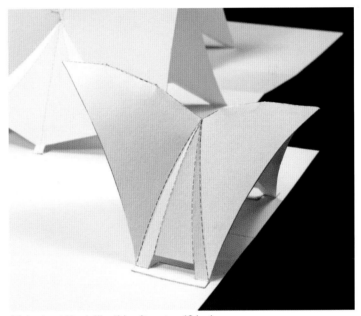

64. It should look like this after step 63 is done.

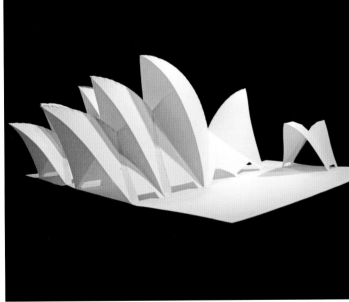

Finished Model.

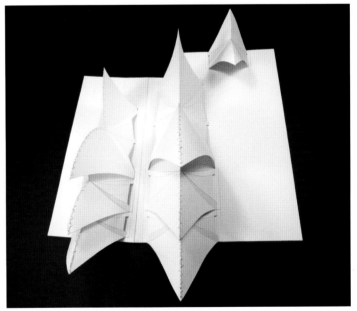

The finished model seen from above.

THE EIFFEL TOWER
Paris, France

Construction of the Eiffel Tower began on January 26, 1887 in celebration of France's centennial celebration of it's revolution in 1889. The main architect was Alexandre Gustave Eiffel, a brilliant engineer and amateur scientist. It was the tallest structure in the world when it was finished. It has a total of 18,038 pieces of wrought iron joined together to create it's now easily recognizable shape. It has a total of 1710 steps to the topmost third level small platform counted from the ground, but the elevator system carries most tourists to the various levels. The names of 72 prominent French scientists and famous personalities are affixed on the sides of Eiffel Tower just beneath the first platform, 18 names per side. Over 200 million people have visited the Eiffel Tower since it opened.

The Eiffel Tower is located on the Champ de Mars in Paris. In terms of height, it stands tall at 1063 feet or 324 meters. Its depth is measured at 328 feet or 100 meters, while its width is 328 feet or 100 meters.

Dimensions of the finished model:
(excluding the baseboard)
7.44 inches or 18.9 cm in length
7.44 inches or 18.9 cm in width
19.2 inches or 48.7 cm in height.

Pieces count: 71 pieces (excluding the baseboard)

Difficulty level: 5/10 (medium)

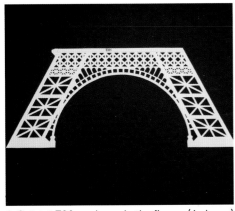

1. Cut out **E01** as shown in the figure. (4 pieces)

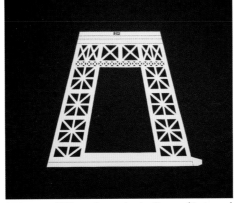

2. Cut out **E02** as shown in the figure. (4 pieces)

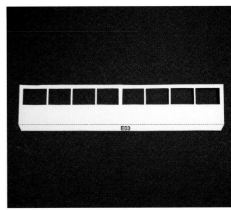

3. Cut out **E03** as shown in the figure. (4 pieces)

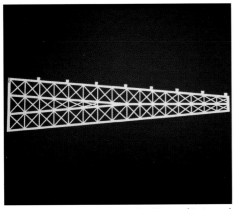

4. Cut out **E04** as shown in the figure. (2 pieces)

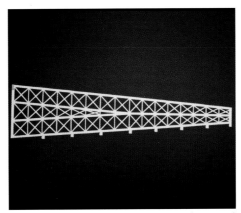

5. Cut out **E05** as shown in the figure. (2 pieces)

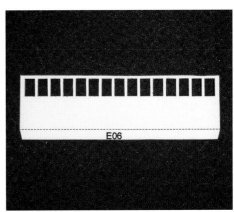

6. Cut out **E06** as shown in the figure. (4 pieces)

7. Cut out **E07** as shown in the figure. (4 pieces)

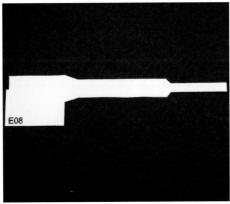

8. Cut out **E08** as shown in the figure.

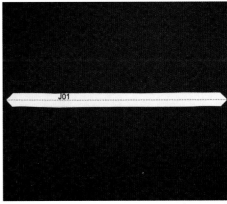

9. Cut out **J01** as shown in the figure. (2 pieces)

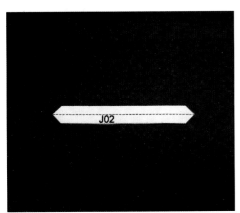

10. Cut out **J02** as shown in the figure. (8 pieces)

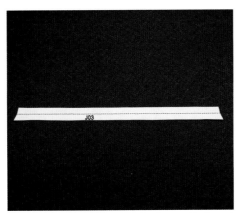

11. Cut out **J03** as shown in the figure. (4 pieces)

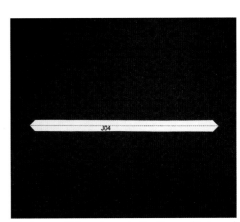

12. Cut out **J04** as shown in the figure. (2 pieces)

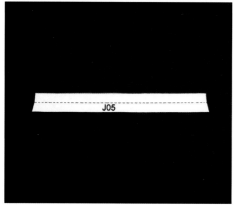

13. Cut out **J05** as shown in the figure. (4 pieces)

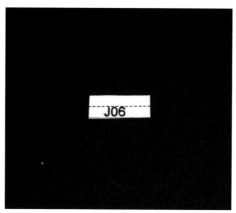

14. Cut out **J06** as shown in the figure. (16 pieces)

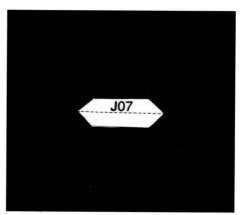

15. Cut out **J07** as shown in the figure. (4 pieces)

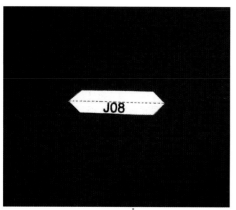

16. Cut out **J08** as shown in the figure. (2 pieces)

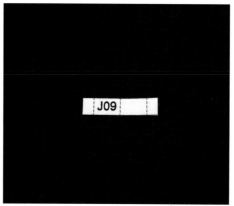

17. Cut out **J09** as shown in the figure. (2 pieces)

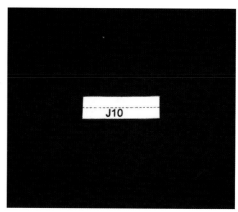

18. Cut out **J10** as shown in the figure. (2 pieces)

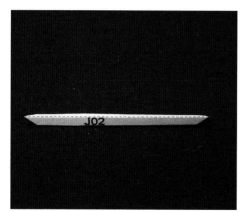

19. Fold all **J02** as shown in the figure.

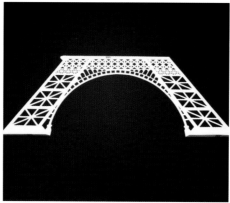

20. Glue two **J02** onto **E01** as shown in the figure.

21. Glue **J03** to join **E01** and E02 as shown in the figure.

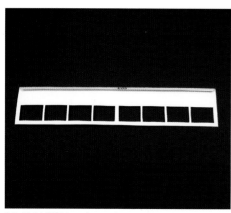

22. Fold **E03** as shown in the figure.

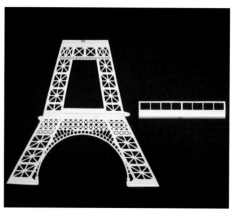

23. Glue **E03** on the top of **J03** as shown in the figure.

24. It should look like this after step 23 done.

25. Repeat step 20 to 23 to make four components total.

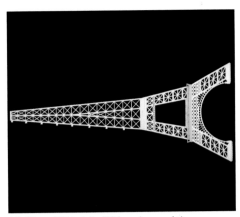

26. Glue **J05** to join **E04** and one of the components shown in step 25.

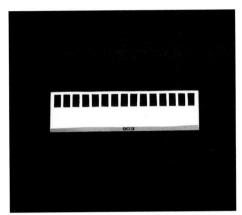

27. Fold **E06** as shown in the figure.

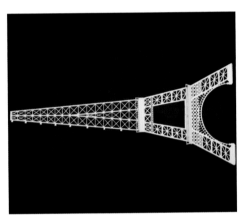

28. Glue **E06** on the top of **J05** as shown in the figure.

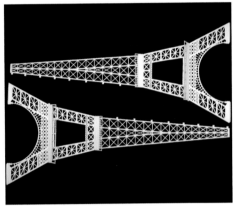

29. Repeat step 26 to 28 to make two components total.

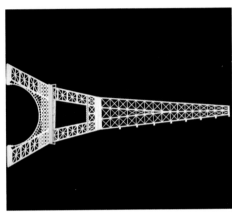

30. Glue **J05** to join **E05** and one of the components shown in step 25.

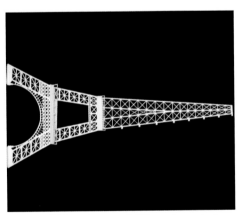

31. Glue **E06** on the top of **J05** as shown in the figure.

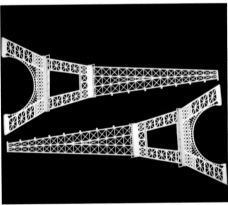

32. Repeat step 30 to 31 to make two components total

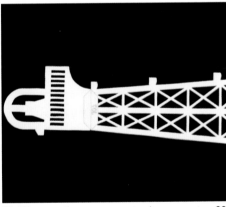

33. Flip over the components shown on step 29 and 32. Glue J07 to join E07 and the top of each component as shown in the figure.

34. It should look like this after step 33 done.

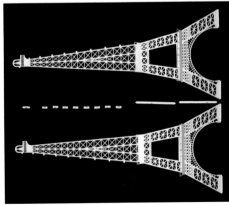

35. Flip over the components first. Glue **J08**, eight **J06**, **J04** and **J01** to join one of each component come from step 29 and 32 as shown in the figure.

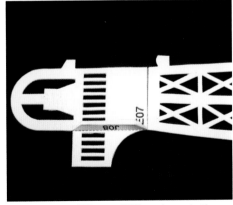

36. First, glue **J08** on to **E07** as shown in the figure.

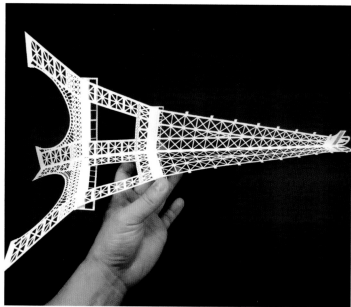

37. It should look like this when it is done.

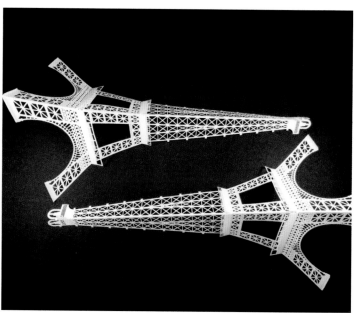

38. Repeat step 35 to 36 to make two components total.

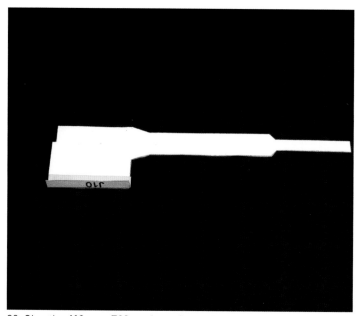

39. Glue the **J10** onto **E08** as shown in the figure.

40. Fold **J09** as shown in the figure. Make two total.

41. Glue one **J09** onto the **E08** as shown in the figure.

42. Glue another **J09** onto the **E08** as shown in the figure.

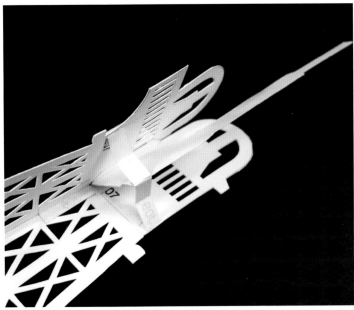

43. Glue the **J10** and two **J09** to one of the unit shown in step 38, as shown in the figure.

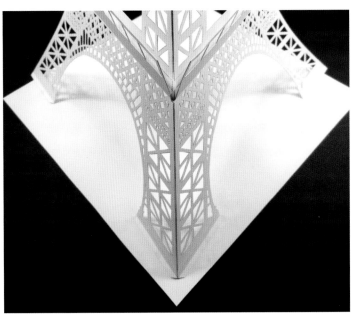

44. Glue it onto the baseboard as shown in the figure.

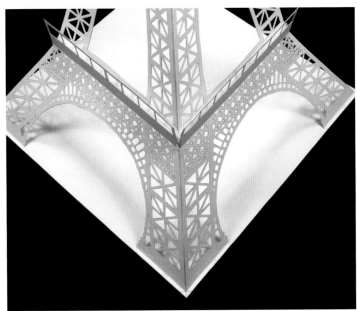

45. It should look like this after step 44 done.

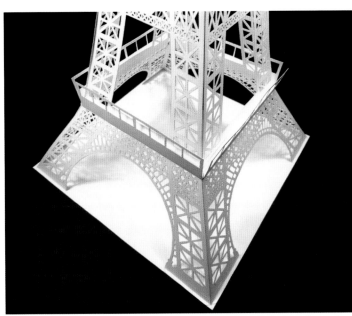

46. Glue another unit shown in step 38 onto the baseboard as shown in the figure.

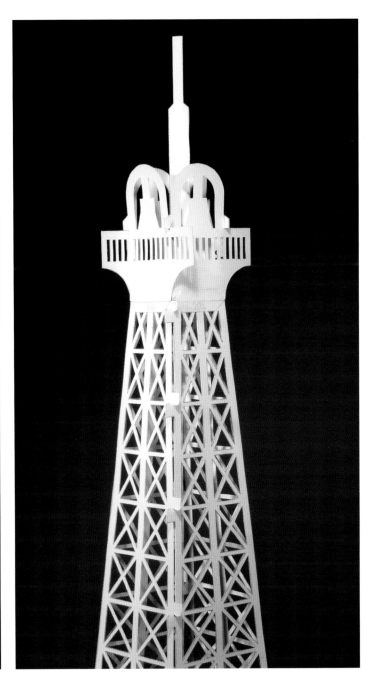

THE OSAKA CASTLE
Osaka, Japan

After defeating the monks who originally lived on this location, the Osaka Tenshu (also called Osaka Castle) was built by Toyotomi Hideyoshi in 1583. It was meant to be a testament to his growing power and prestige in Japan. Hideyoshi was the "great unifier" of Japan and his rule was marked by great accomplishments by the people of Japan. To protect the castle from attack, it was surrounded by a moat with only two small bridges with access to the castle grounds. Several turrets were built around the main building as a first line of defense against attack, and the main building was bristling with defenses. Due to the calamities of war and civil strife, the original castle no longer stands, but the reconstructed building holds true to Hideyoshi's original construction. Now a museum in the middle of 185 acres of Osaka's most beautiful park, Osaka Castle is a majestic testimony to a glorious era in Japan's history.

The Osaka Castle is located in the center of the city of Osaka Japan. It's 102 feet tall on a 75 foot stone base.

Dimensions of the finished model:
(excluding the baseboard)
8.14 inches or 20.7 cm in length
8.14 inches or 20.7 cm in width
9.35 inches or 23.7 cm in height.

Pieces count: 144 pieces (excluding the baseboard)

Difficulty level: 5/10 (medium)

1. Cut out **Y01** as shown in the figure. (2 pieces)

2. Cut out **Y02** as shown in the figure. (2 pieces)

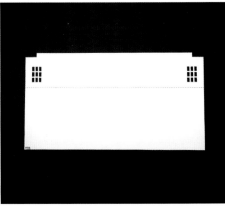

3. Cut out **Y03** as shown in the figure. (2 pieces)

4. Cut out **Y04** as shown in the figure. (2 pieces)

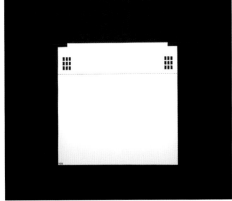

5. Cut out **Y05** as shown in the figure. (2 pieces)

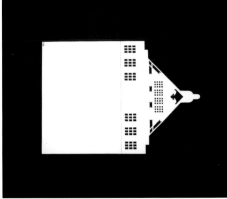

6. Cut out **Y06** as shown in the figure. (2 pieces)

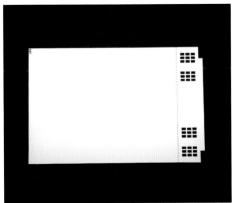

7. Cut out **Y07** as shown in the figure. (2 pieces)

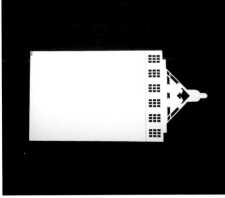

8. Cut out **Y08** as shown in the figure. (2 pieces)

9. Cut out **Y09** as shown in the figure. (4 pieces)

10. Cut out **Y11** as shown in the figure. (4 pieces)

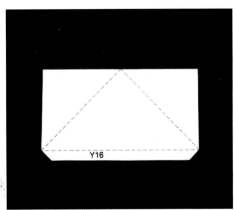

11. Cut out **Y16** as shown in the figure. (2 pieces)

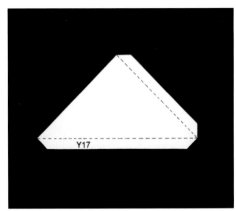

12. Cut out **Y17** as shown in the figure. (2 pieces)

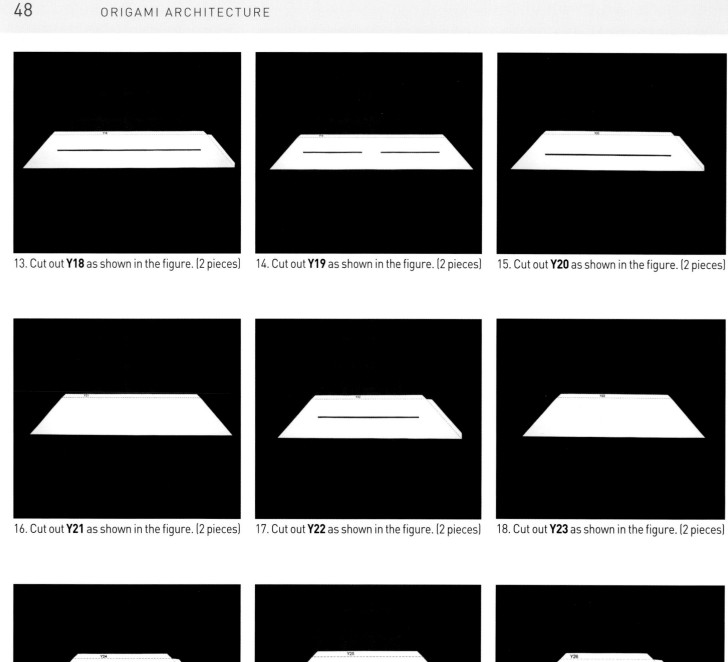

13. Cut out **Y18** as shown in the figure. (2 pieces)

14. Cut out **Y19** as shown in the figure. (2 pieces)

15. Cut out **Y20** as shown in the figure. (2 pieces)

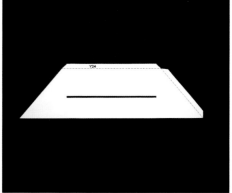

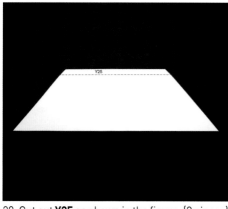

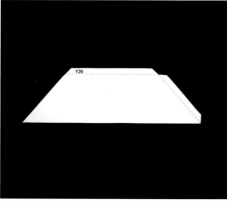

16. Cut out **Y21** as shown in the figure. (2 pieces)

17. Cut out **Y22** as shown in the figure. (2 pieces)

18. Cut out **Y23** as shown in the figure. (2 pieces)

19. Cut out **Y24** as shown in the figure. (2 pieces)

20. Cut out **Y25** as shown in the figure. (2 pieces)

21. Cut out **Y26** as shown in the figure. (2 pieces)

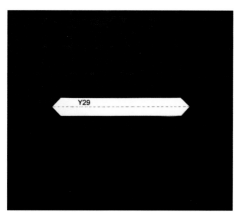

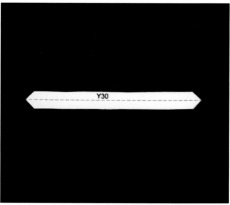

22. Cut out **Y27** as shown in the figure. (2 pieces)

23. Cut out **Y29** as shown in the figure. (4 pieces)

24. Cut out **Y30** as shown in the figure. (4 pieces)

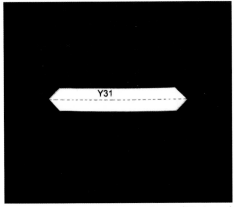

25. Cut out **Y31** as shown in the figure. (88 pieces)

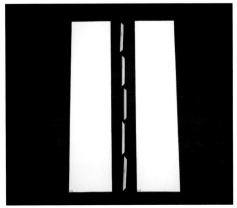

26. Glue five pieces of **Y31** to join two pieces **Y11** as shown in the figure.

27. It should look like this after step 25 done.

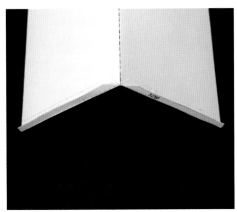

28. Glue two pieces of **Y29** on it as shown in the figure.

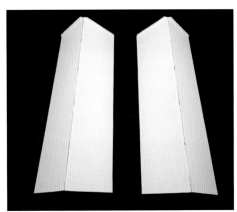

29. Repeat step 26 to 28 to make two components.

30. Glue four pieces of **Y31** to join two pieces **Y09** as shown in the figure.

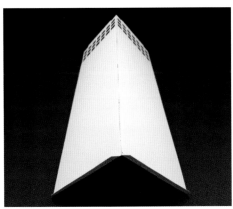

31. Glue two pieces of **Y30** on it as shown in the figure.

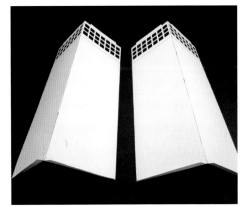

32. Repeat step 30 to 31 to make two components total.

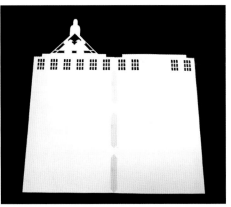

33. Glue three pieces of **Y31** to join **Y07** and **Y08** as shown in the figure.

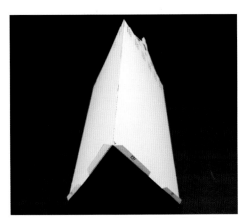

34. Glue four pieces of **Y31** on it as shown in the figure.

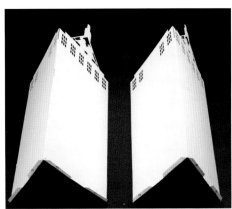

35. Repeat step 33 to 34 to make two components total.

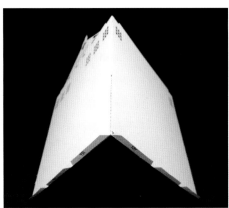

36. Glue three pieces of **Y31** to join **Y05** and **Y06**. Glue six pieces of **Y31** at the bottom as shown in the figure.

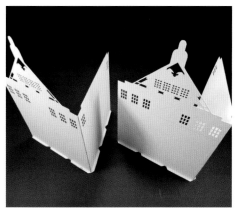

37. Repeat step 36 to make two components total.

38. Glue two pieces of **Y31** to join **Y03** and **Y04** as shown in the figure.

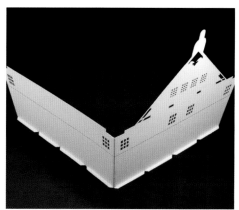

39. Glue eight pieces of **Y31** at the bottom as shown in the figure.

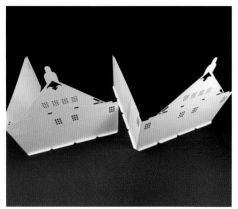

40. Repeat step 38 to 39 to make two components total.

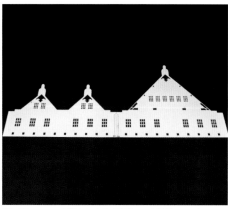

41. Glue one **Y31** to join **Y01** and **Y02** as shown in the figure.

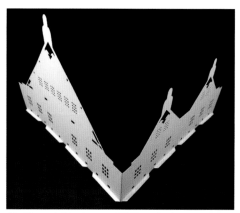

42. Glue eight pieces of **Y31** at the bottom as shown in the figure.

43. Repeat step 41 to 42 to make two components total.

44. Fold the **Y18** as shown in the figure.

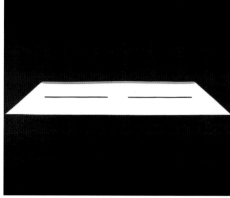

45. Fold the **Y19** as shown in the figure.

46. Apply glue on the folding edge to join two pieces together as shown in the figure.

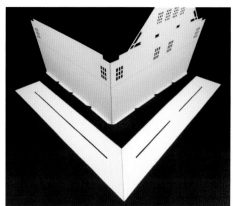

47. Take one component from step 40. Apply glue on the folding edge to join two units together as shown in the figure.

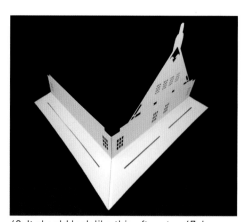

48. It should look like this after step 47 done.

49. Fold the **Y21** as shown in the figure.

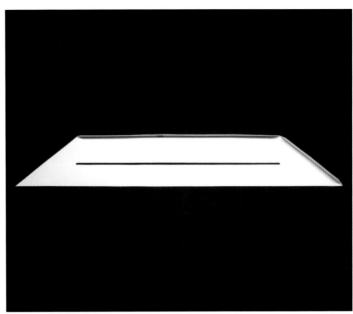

50. Fold the **Y20** as shown in the figure. Apply glue on the folded edge to join with **Y23** together.

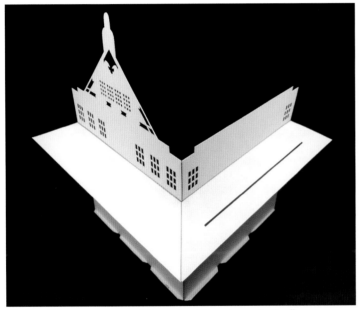

51. Glue it to one component from step 37 as shown in the figure.

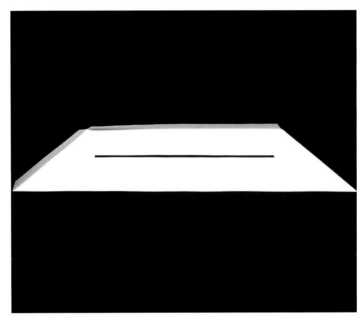

52. Fold the **Y22** as shown in the figure.

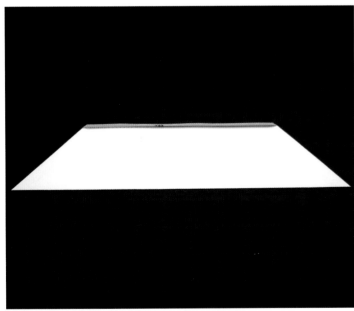

53. Fold the **Y23** as shown in the figure.

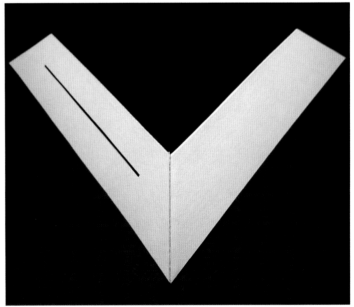

54. Apply glue on the folding edge to join two pieces together as shown in the figure.

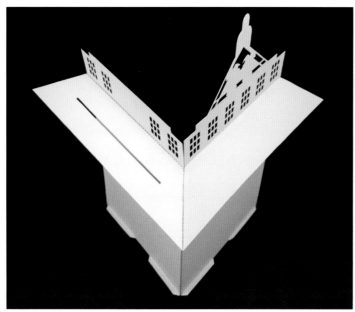

55. Take one component from step 35. Apply glue on the folded edge to join two units together as shown in the figure.

56. Fold the **Y24** as shown in the figure.

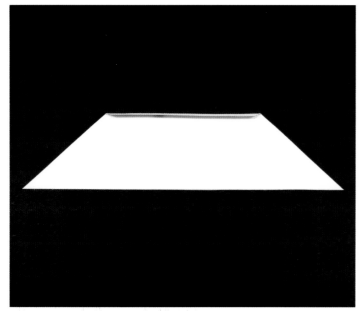

57. Fold the **Y25** as shown in the figure.

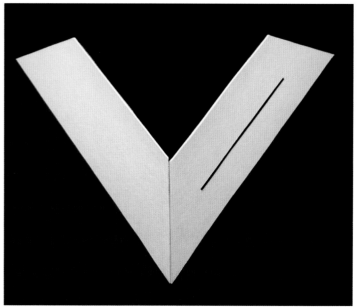

58. Apply glue on the folding edge to join two pieces together as shown in the figure.

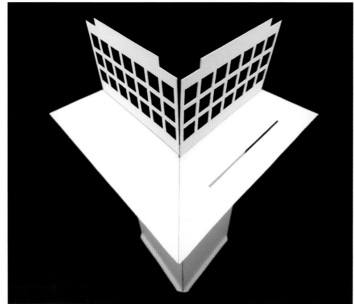

59. Take one component from step 35. Apply glue on the folding edge to join two units together as shown in the figure.

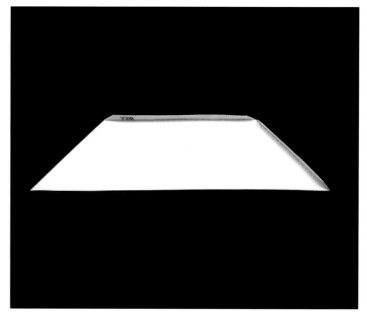

60. Fold the **Y26** as shown in the figure.

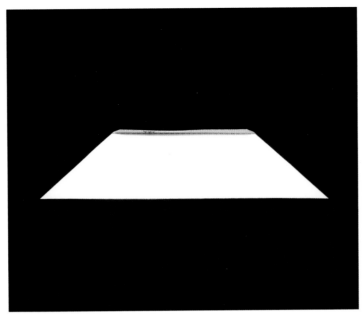

61. Fold the **Y27** as shown in the figure.

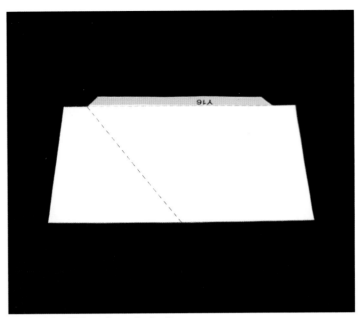

62. Fold the **Y16** as shown in the figure.

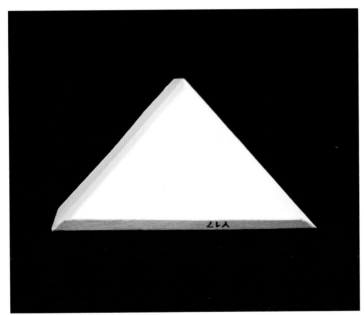

63. Fold the **Y17** as shown in the figure.

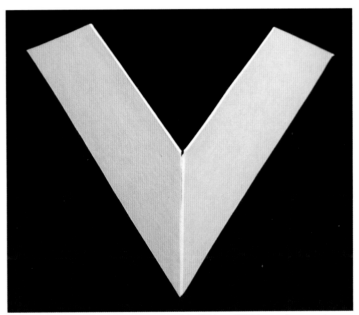

64. Apply glue on the folded edge to join **Y26** and **Y27** together as shown in the figure.

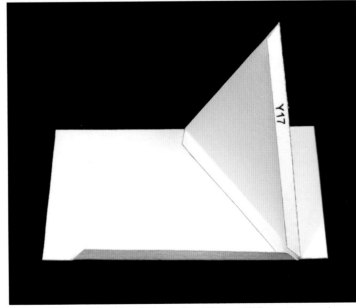

65. Apply glue on the folded edge to join **Y16** and **Y17** together as shown in the figure.

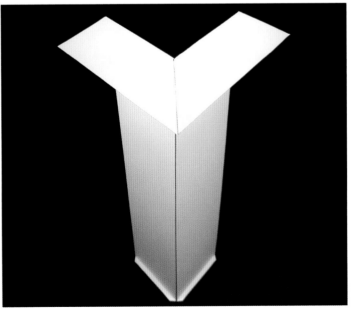

66. Take one component from step 29 and the component from step 64. Apply glue on the folded edge to join two units together as shown in the figure.

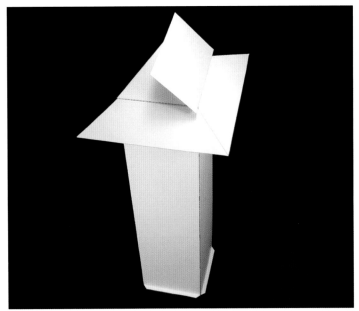

67. Take the component from step 65. Apply glue on the folded edge to join two units together as shown in the figure.

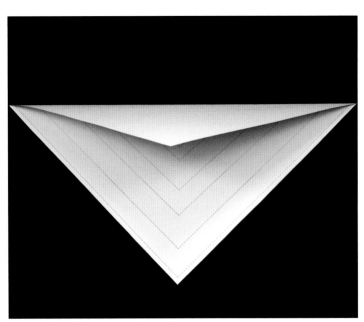

68. Fold the **Y32** as shown in the figure.

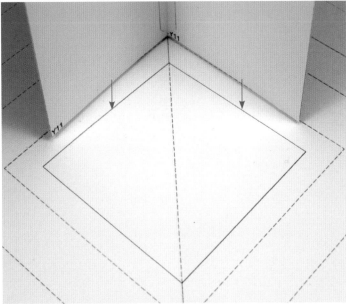

69. Take the component in step 67. Use glue on the folded edge and cohere as shown in the figure.

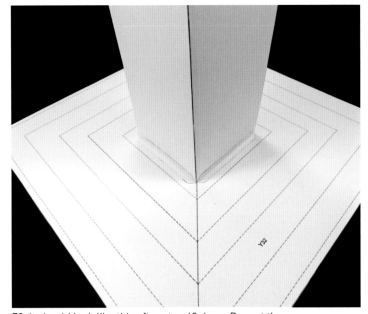

70. It should look like this after step 69 done. Repeat the same procedure to make another identical unit as shown in step 67.

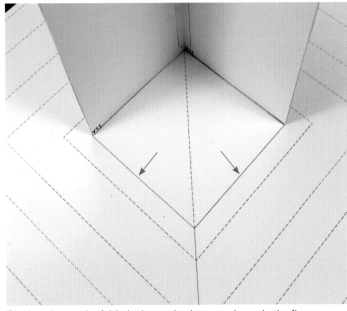

71. Use glue on the folded edge and cohere as shown in the figure.

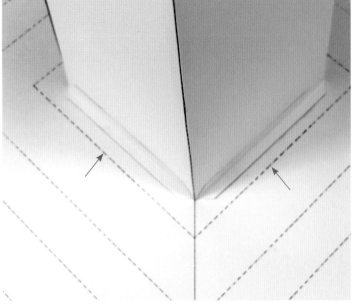

72. Take the component in step 59. Use glue on the folded edge and cohere as shown in the figure.

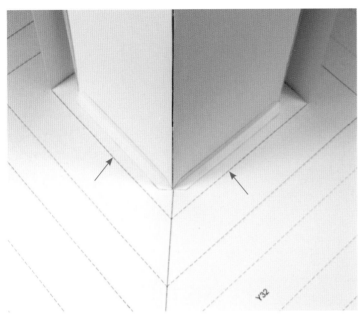

73. It should look like this after step 72 is done. Repeat the same procedure to make another identical unit as shown in step 59.

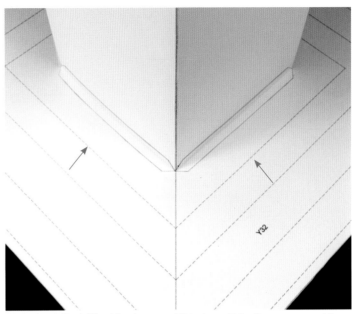

74. It should look like this after step 73 is done. Take the component from step 55. Use glue on the folded edge and cohere as shown in the figure.

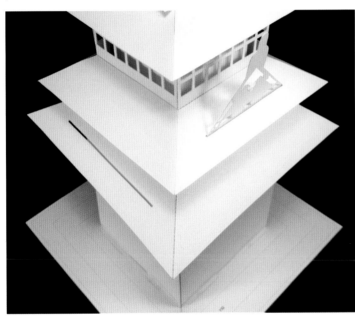

75. Tuck the piece through the slot as shown in the figure.

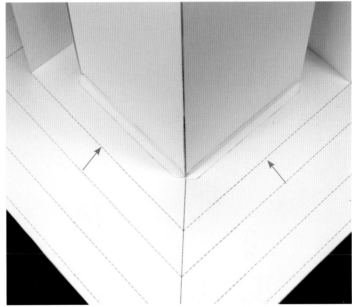

76. Repeat the same procedure to make another identical unit as shown in step 55. Use glue on the folded edge and cohere as shown in the figure.

77. Tuck the piece through the slot as shown in the figure. It should look like this after step 76 is done.

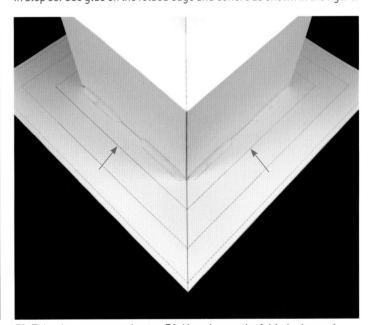

78. Take the component in step 51. Use glue on the folded edge and cohere as shown in the figure.

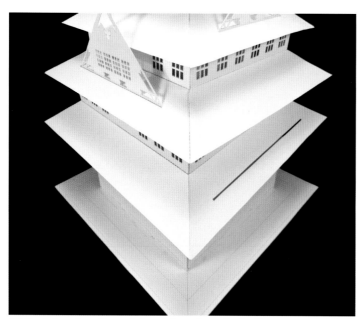

79. Tuck the piece through the slot as shown in the figure.

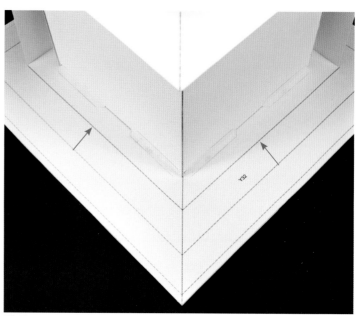

80. Repeat the same procedure to make another identical unit as shown in step 51. Use glue on the folded edge and cohere as shown in the figure.

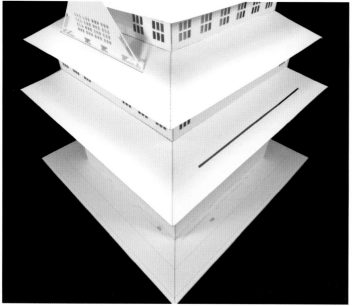

81. Tuck the piece through the slot as shown in the figure. It should look like this after step 80 done.

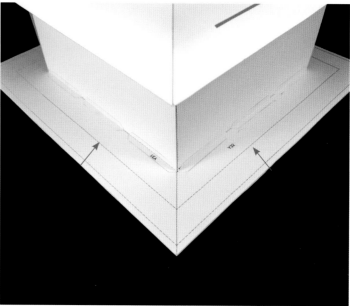

82. Take the component from step 48. Use glue on the folded edge and cohere as shown in the figure.

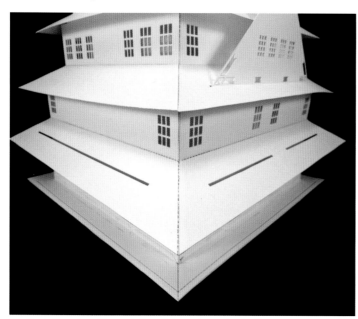

83. Tuck the piece through the slot as shown in the figure.

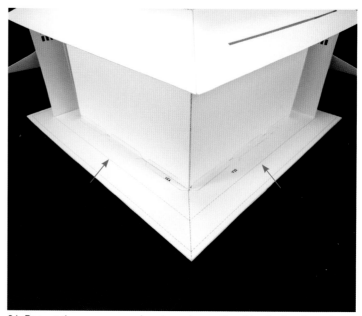

84. Repeat the same procedure to make another identical unit as shown in step 48. Use glue on the folded edge and cohere as shown in the figure.

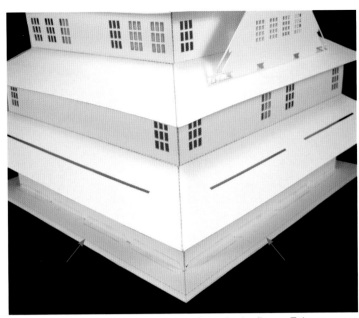

85. Tuck the piece through the slot as shown in the figure. Take one component in step 43. Glue the folded edge and cohere as shown above.

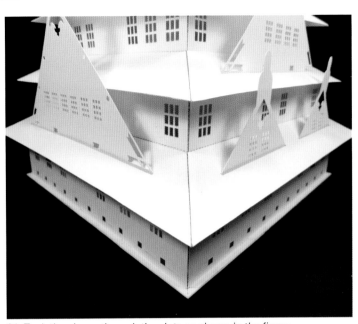

86. Tuck the pieces through the slots as shown in the figure.

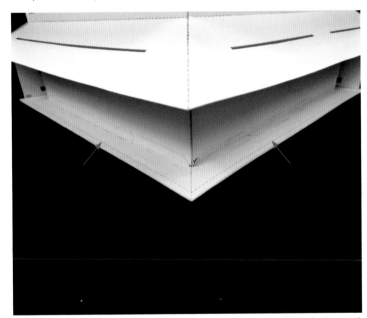

87. Take another component in step 43. Use glue on the folded edge and cohere as shown in the figure.

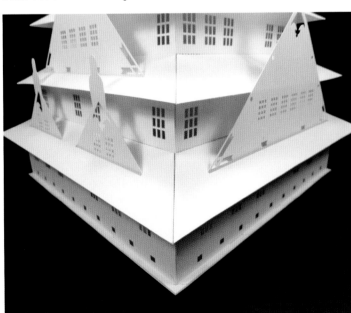

88. Tuck the pieces through the slots as shown in the figure.

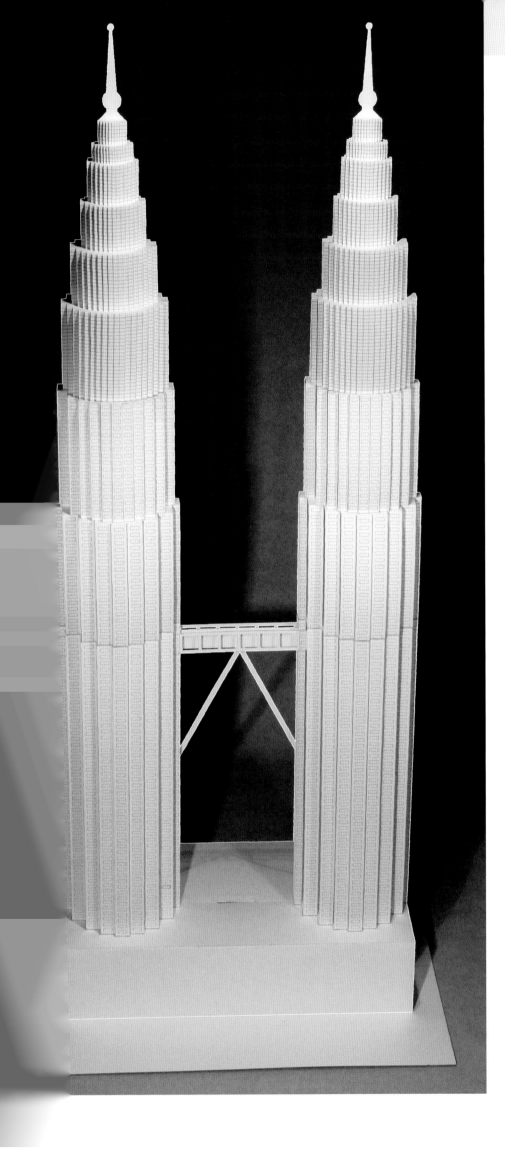

PETRONAS TOWERS
Kuala Lumpur, Malaysia

Designed by Argentine-American architects César Pelli and Djay Cerico under the consultancy of Julius Gold, the Petronas Towers were completed in August 1998 after a seven year build. It became the tallest building in the world on the date of its completion. Designed to embody the past and future of Malaysia, the Petronas Towers was given the Aga Khan Award for Architecture in 2004. The Skybridge, a major attraction at the Petronas Twin Towers, is a double-decked bridge at the 41st and 42nd floors. It is used to facilitate movement between the two towers and as an observation area. A city within a city, the Petronas Towers has a symphonic concert hall between the buildings, an art gallery, a science discovery center, and adjoins the Suria KLCC Mall.

The Petronas Towers is located in Kuala Lumpur, Malaysia. In terms of height, it stands tall at 1483 feet or 452 meters.

Dimensions of the finished model:
(exclude baseboard)
8.42 inches or 21.4 cm in length
4.77 inches or 12.1 cm in width
22.1 inches or 56.1 cm in height.

Pieces count: 46 pieces (exclude baseboard)

Difficulty level: 6/10 (medium)

All the blue line is folding line.

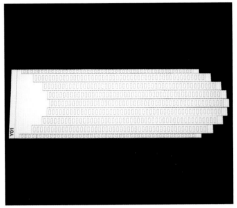

1. Cut out **Y01** as shown in the figure. (2 pieces)

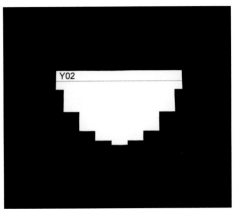

2. Cut out **Y02** as shown in the figure. (6 pieces)

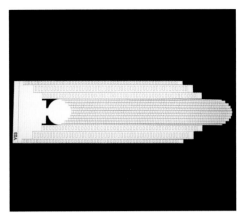

3. Cut out **Y03** as shown in the figure. (2 pieces)

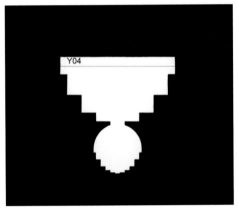

4. Cut out **Y04** as shown in the figure. (2 pieces)

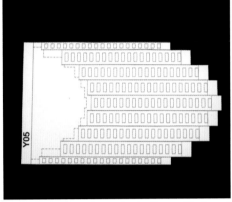

5. Cut out **Y05** as shown in the figure. (4 pieces)

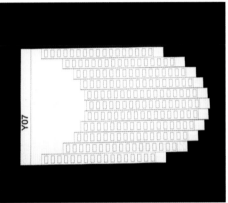

6. Cut out **Y07** as shown in the figure. (4 pieces)

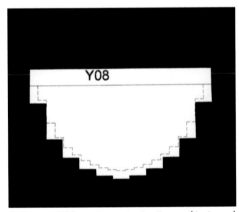

7. Cut out **Y08** as shown in the figure. (4 pieces)

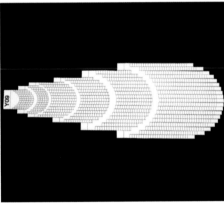

8. Cut out **Y09** as shown in the figure. (4 pieces)

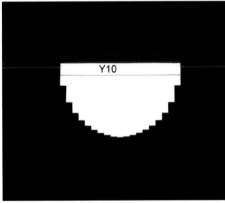

9. Cut out **Y10** as shown in the figure. (4 pieces)

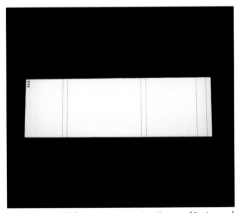

10. Cut out **Y11** as shown in the figure. (2 pieces)

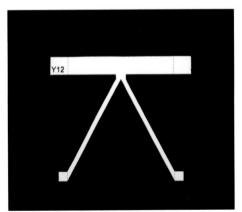

11. Cut out **Y12** as shown in the figure.

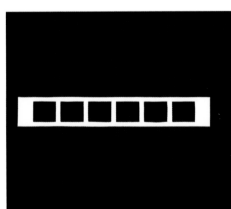

12. Cut out **Y13** as shown in the figure. (2 pieces)

13. Cut out **Y14** as shown in the figure. (2 pieces)

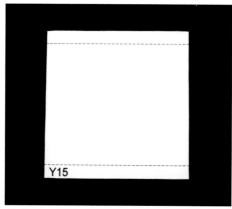

14. Cut out **Y15** as shown in the figure. (2 pieces)

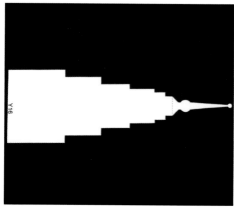

15. Cut out **Y16** as shown in the figure. (2 pieces)

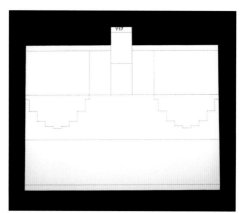

16. Cut out **Y17** as shown in the figure.

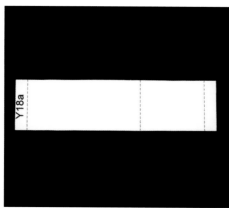

17. Cut out **Y18a** as shown in the figure.

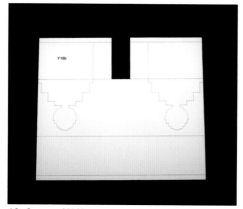

18. Cut out **Y18b** as shown in the figure.

19. Fold the upper part of **Y01** as shown in the figure.

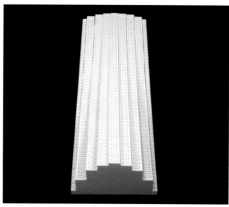

20. Fold other parts of **Y01** as shown in the figure.

21. Fold the lower part of **Y01** as shown in the figure.

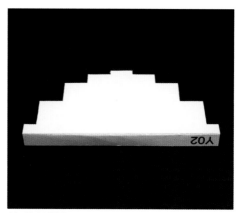

22. Fold **Y02** as shown in the figure.

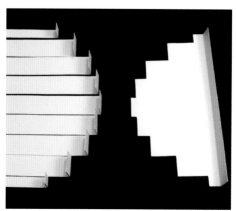

23. Apply glue to join **Y01** and **Y02**.

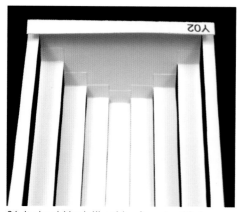

24. It should look like this after step 23 done.

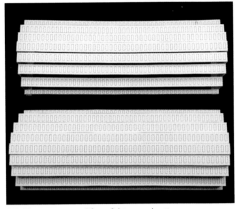

25. Repeat step 19 to 24 to make two components total.

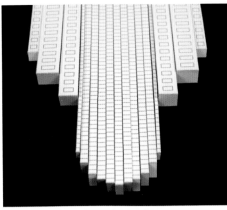

26. Fold **Y03** as shown in the figure.

27. Apply glue to join **Y03** and **Y04**.

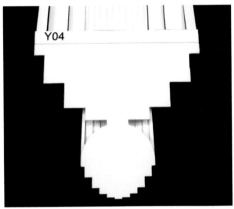

28. It should look like this after **Y03** and **Y04** are joined.

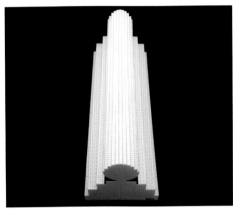

29. Fold the unit as shown in the figure.

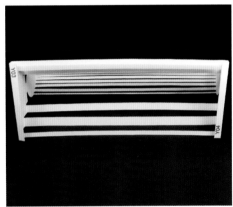

30. Fold the edges as shown in the figure.

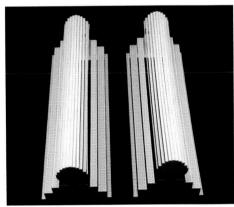

31. Repeat step 26 to 30 to make two components total.

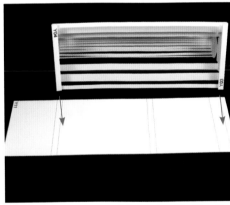

32. Take one component from step 31. Glue it onto **Y11** as shown in the figure.

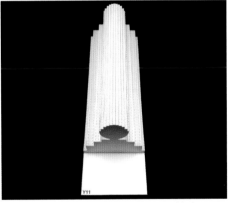

33. It should look like this after step 32 done.

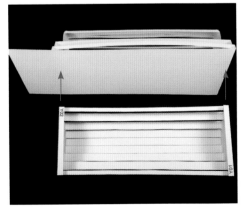

34. Take one component from step 25. Glue it onto **Y11** as shown in the figure.

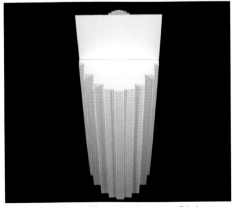

35. It should look like this after step 34 done.

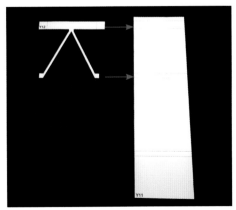

36. Glue **Y12** to **Y11** as shown in the figure.

37. Take one component from step 31. Glue it onto **Y11** as shown in the figure.

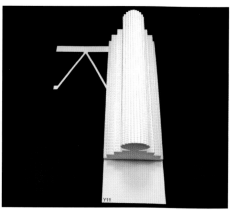

38. It should look like this after step 37 done.

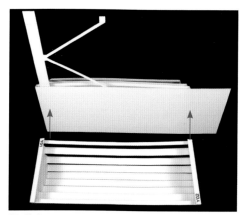

39. Take one component from step 25. Glue it onto **Y11** as shown in the figure.

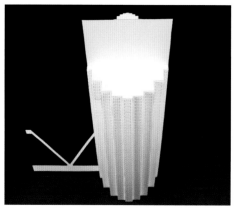

40. It should look like this after step 39 done.

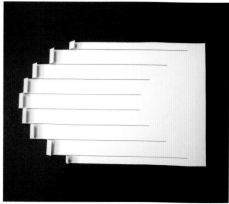

41. Fold **Y05** as shown in the figure.

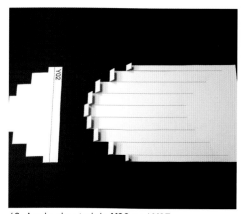

42. Apply glue to join **Y02** and **Y05**

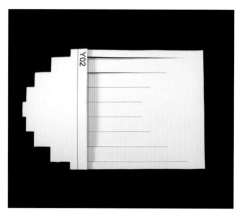

43. It should look like this after step 42 done.

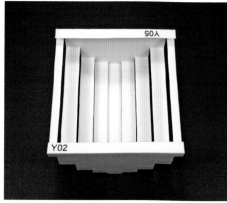

44. Fold the unit as shown in the figure.

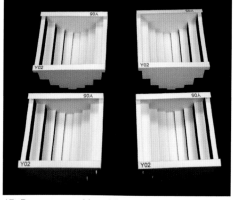

45. Repeat step 41 to 44 to make four components total.

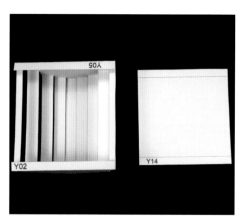

46. Take one component from step 45. Glue it to **Y14** as shown in the figure.

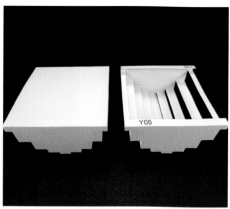

47. Take another component from step 45. Glue it to **Y14** as shown in the figure.

48. It should look like this after step 47 done.

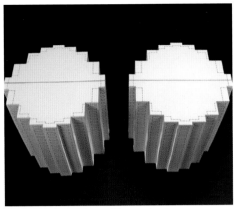

49. Repeat step 46 to 47 to make two components total.

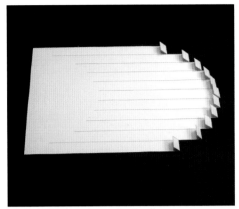

50. Fold **Y07** as shown in the figure.

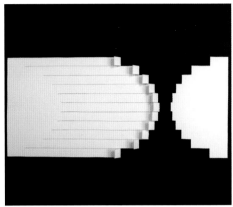

51. Apply glue to join **Y07** and **Y08**.

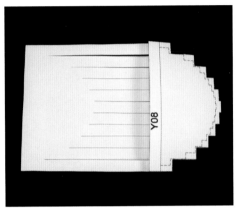

52. It should look like this after step 51 done.

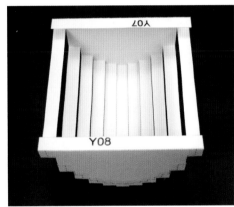

53. Fold the unit as shown in the figure.

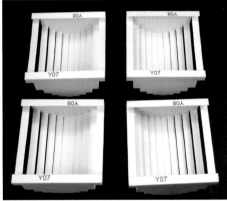

54. Repeat step 50 to 53 to make four components total.

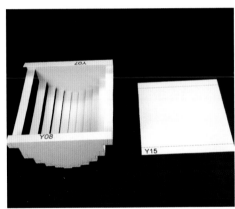

55. Take one component from step 54. Glue it to **Y15** as shown in the figure.

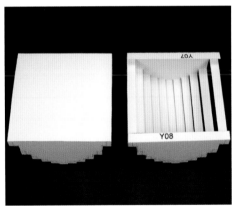

56. Take another component from step 54. Glue it to **Y15** as shown in the figure.

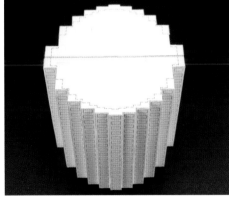

57. It should look like this after step 56 done.

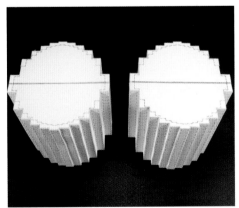

58. Repeat step 55 to 56 to make two components total.

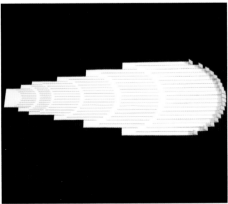

59. Fold **Y09** as shown in the figure.

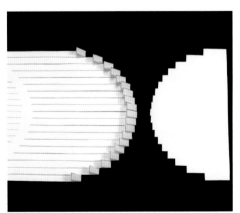

60. Apply glue to join **Y09** and **Y10**.

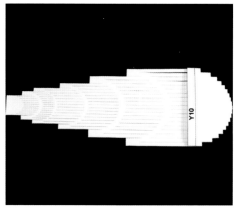

61. It should look like this after step 60 done.

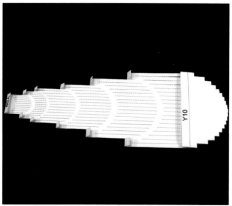

62. Fold the gluing edges as shown in the figure.

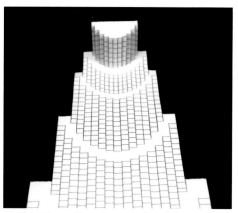

63. Fold the unit as shown in the figure.

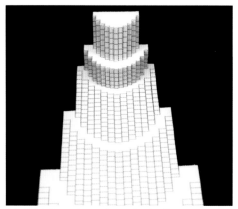

64. Fold the unit as shown in the figure.

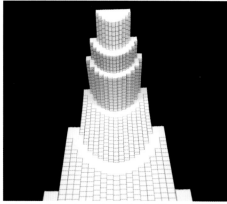

65. Fold the unit as shown in the figure.

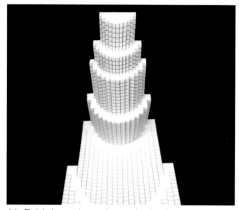

66. Fold the unit as shown in the figure.

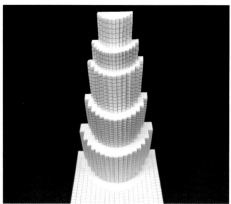

67. Fold the unit as shown in the figure.

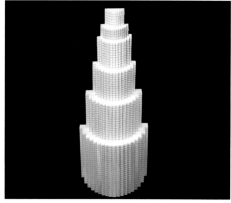

68. Fold the unit as shown in the figure.

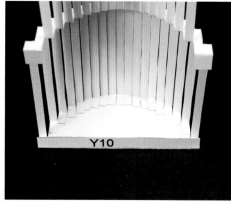

69. Fold the gluing edge as shown in the figure.

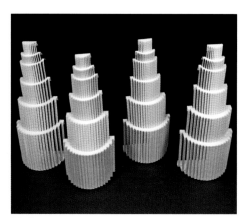

70. Repeat step 59 to 69 to make four components total

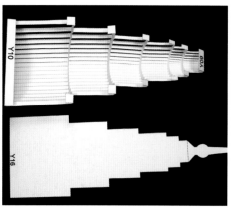

71. Take one component from step 70. Glue it to **Y16** as shown in the figure.

72. It should look like this after step 71 done.

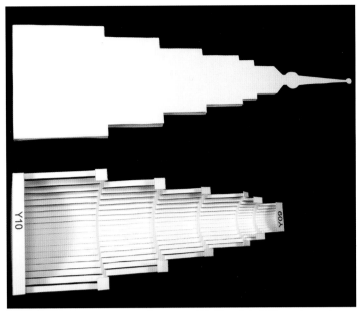

73. Take another component from step 70. Glue it to **Y16** as shown in the figure.

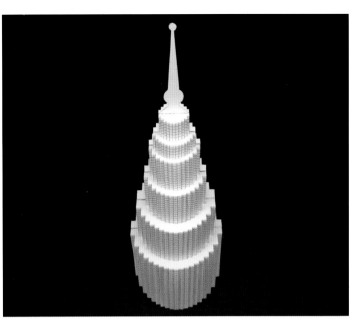

74. It should look like this after step 73 done.

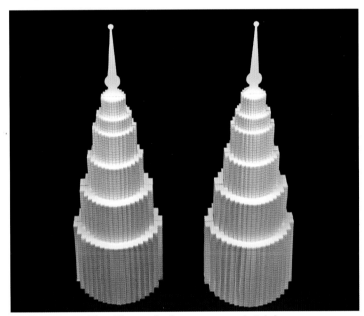

75. Repeat step 71 to 73 to make four components total.

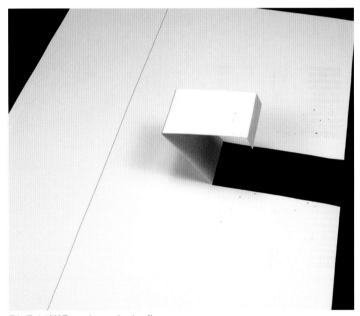

76. Fold **Y17** as shown in the figure.

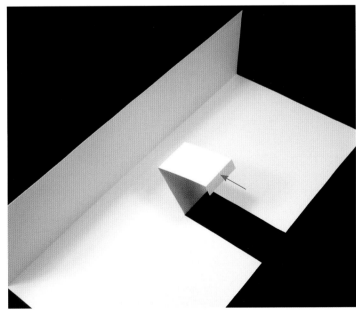

77. Fold **Y17** as shown in the figure. Apply glue as shown in the figure.

78. Close it tightly. The folded edges will find a perfect position to be glued.

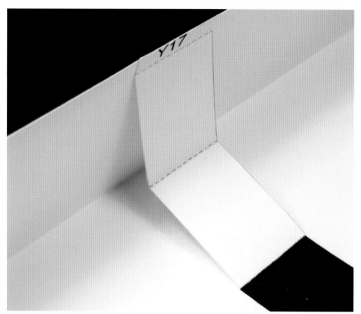

79. It should look like this after step 78 done.

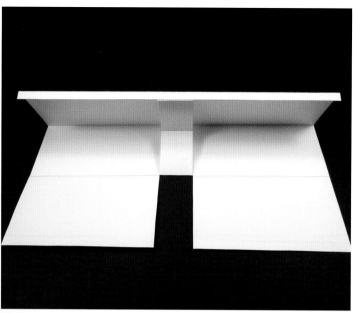

80. Fold the edge as shown in the figure.

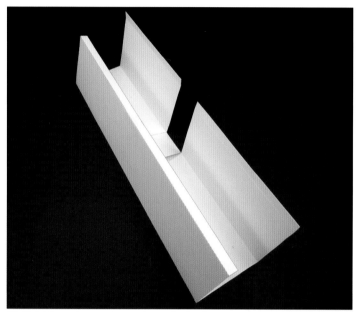

81. Fold these two parts as shown in the figure.

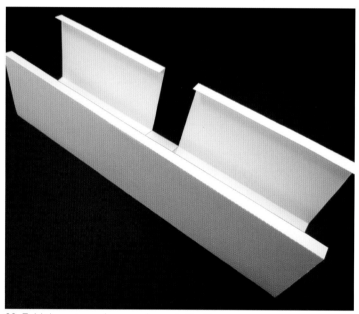

82. Fold these two edges as shown in the figure.

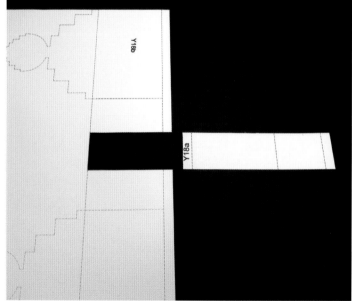

83. Glue to join **Y18a** and **Y18b** together as shown in the figure.

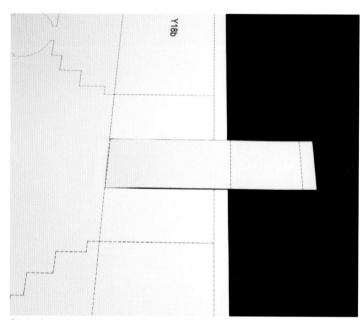

84. It should look like this after step 83 done.

85. Fold **Y18a** as shown in the figure.

86. Fold **Y18b** as shown in the figure. Apply glue as shown in the figure.

87. Close it tightly. The folded piece will find a perfect position to be glued.

88. It should look like this after step 87 done.

89. Fold the edge as shown in the figure.

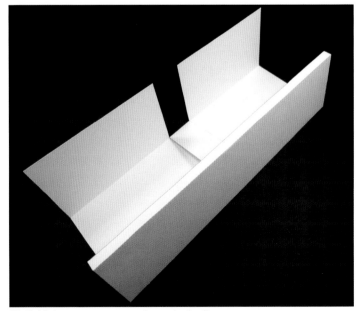

90. Fold these two parts as shown in the figure.

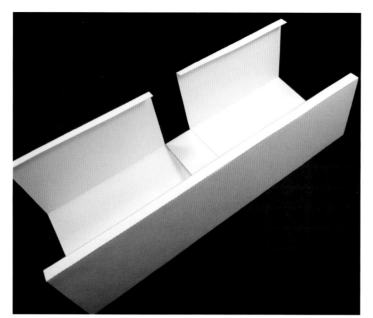

91. Fold the edges as shown in the figure.

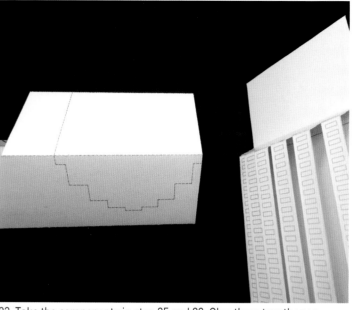

92. Take the components in step 35 and 82. Glue them together as shown in the figure.

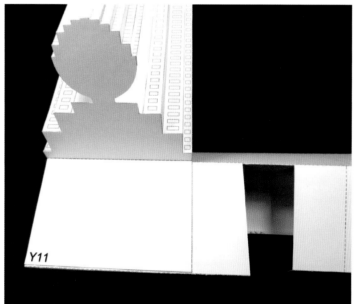

93. It should look like this after step 92 done.

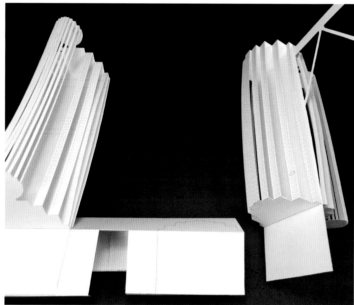

94. Take the component in step 40. Glue them together as shown in the figure.

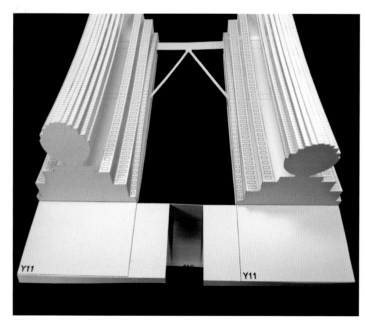

95. It should look like this after step 94 done.

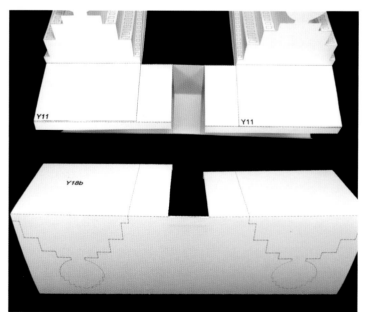

96. Take the component in step 91. Glue them together as shown in the figure.

97. Apply glue and cohere as shown in the figure.

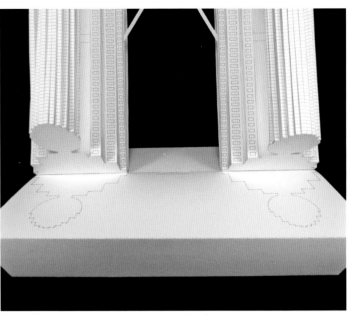

98. Apply glue and cohere as shown in the figure.

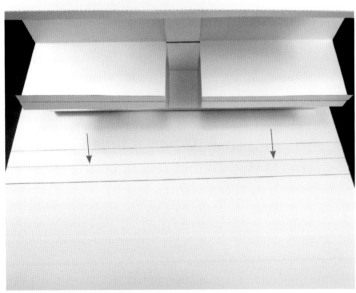

99. Apply glue and cohere as shown in the figure.

100. It should look like this after step 99 done. Apply glue as shown in the figure.

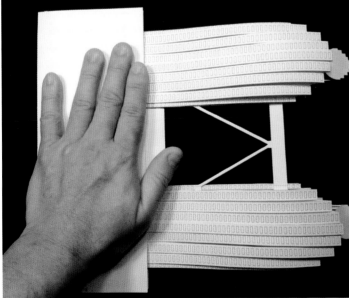

101. Close the baseboard tightly. The folded edge will find a perfect position to be glued.

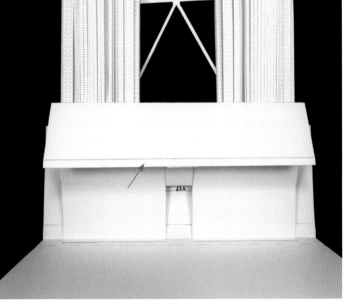

102. Rotate the building 180-degree. Apply glue as shown in the figure.

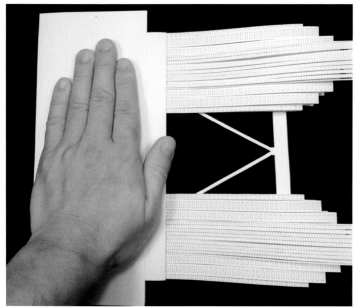

103. Close the baseboard tightly. The folded edge will find a perfect position to be glued.

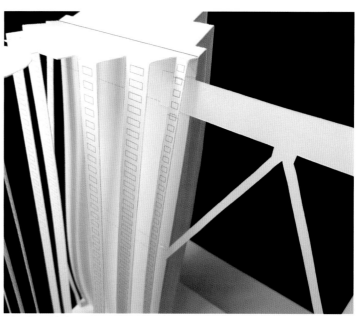

104. Glue **Y12** to **Y11** as shown in the figure.

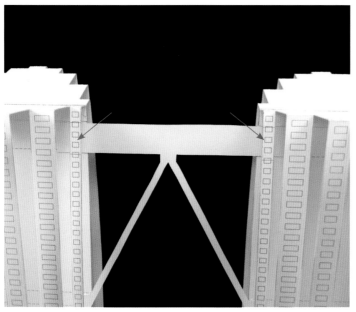

105. Glue **Y13** as shown in the figure.

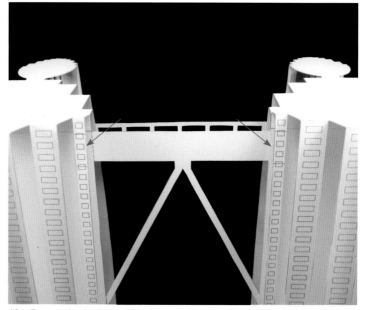

106. Rotate the building 180-degree. Glue another **Y13** as shown in the figure.

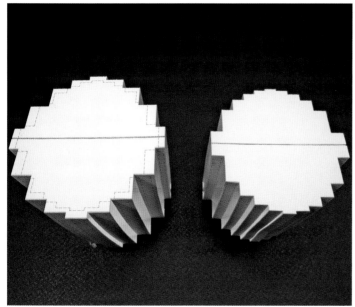

107. Take one component in step 58 and 49. Apply glue to join them together as shown in the figure.

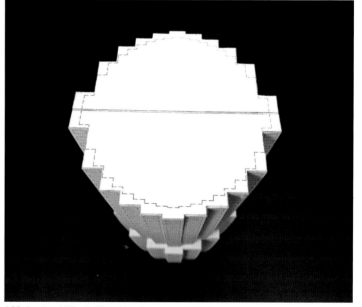

108. It should look like this after step 107 done. Take one component from step 75. Glue it on the top.

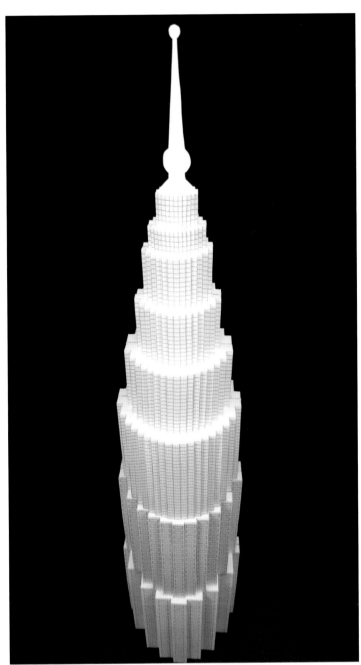

109. It should look like this after step 108 done.

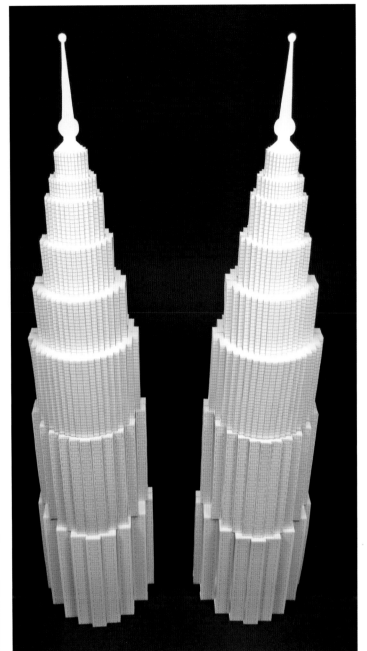

110. Repeat step 107 to 108 to make two components total

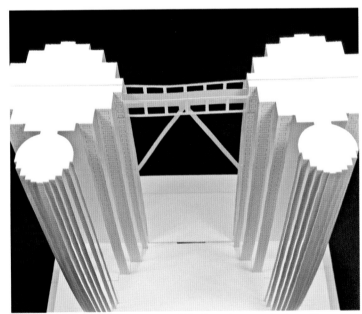

111. Take two components in step 110. Glue them on the top of two buildings as shown in the figure.

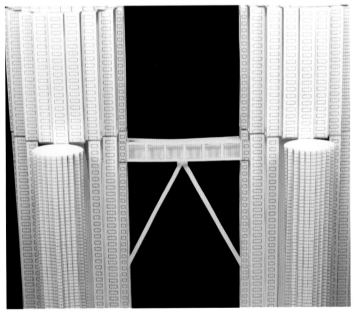

112. It should look like this after step 111 done.

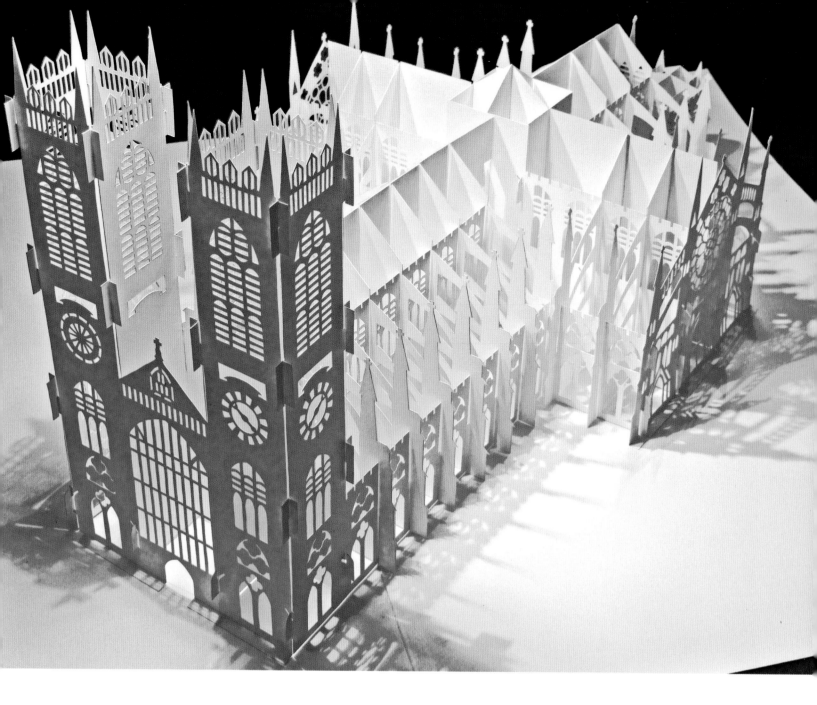

WESTMINSTER ABBEY
London, England

Westminster Abbey was built around 1045–1050 by King Edward the Confessor as part of his palace and was consecrated on 28 December 1065. It was King Henry III in 1265 who built most of what is seen as Westminster Abbey today. Created in traditional Gothic style, the abbey has been the setting for every Coronation of England's monarch since 1066, including the world wide televised coronation of Queen Elizabeth II. The abbey is also the burial place of 17 kings, also the resting place of other noted statesmen, poets, scientists, musicians, aristocrats, admirals, and politicians. A treasure trove of art both old and new, it contains around 600 monuments, statues, and wall tablets. The marriage of Prince William and Kate Middleton took place there in 2011.

Westminster Abbey is located just to the west of the Palace of Westminster, in London, England. In terms of height, it stands tall at 225.3 feet or 68.7 meters. Its depth is measured at 203.2 feet or 61.9 meters, while its width is 530 feet or 161.5 meters.

Dimensions of the finished model:
(excluding the baseboard)
16.48 inches or 41.8 cm in length
8.58 inches or 21.8 cm in width
8.04 inches or 20.4 cm in height.

Pieces count: 37 pieces (excluding the baseboard)

Difficulty level: 6/10 (medium)

Interlock pieces: Assemble the building without glue (excluding the baseboard).

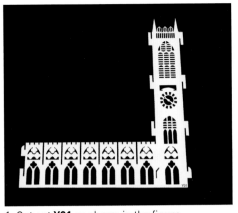

1. Cut out **Y01** as shown in the figure.

2. Cut out **Y02** as shown in the figure.

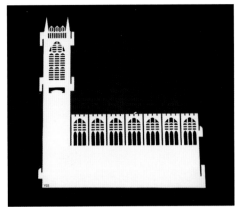

3. Cut out **Y03** as shown in the figure. (2 pieces)

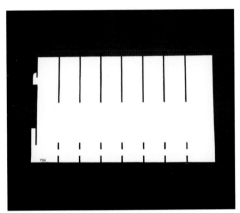

4. Cut out **Y04** as shown in the figure.

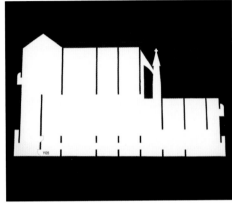

5. Cut out **Y05** as shown in the figure.

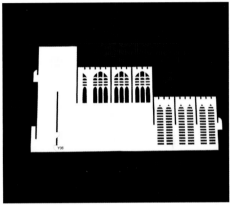

6. Cut out **Y06** as shown in the figure. (2 pieces)

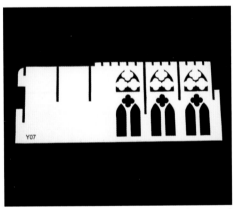

7. Cut out **Y07** as shown in the figure. (2 pieces)

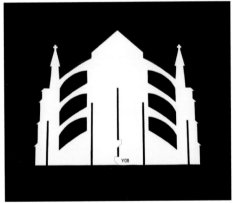

8. Cut out **Y08** as shown in the figure. (4 pieces)

9. Cut out **Y09** as shown in the figure.

10. Cut out **Y10** as shown in the figure.

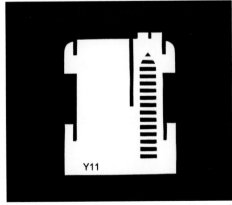

11. Cut out **Y11** as shown in the figure. (2 pieces)

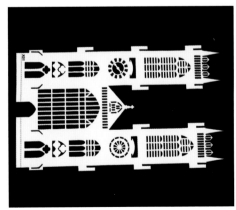

12. Cut out **X01** as shown in the figure.

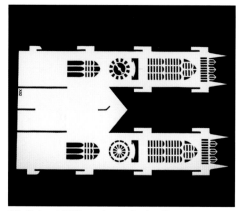

13. Cut out **X02** as shown in the figure.

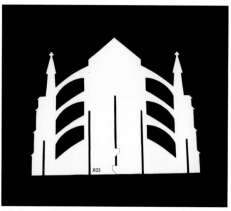

14. Cut out **X03** as shown in the figure. (7 pieces)

15. Cut out **X04** as shown in the figure.

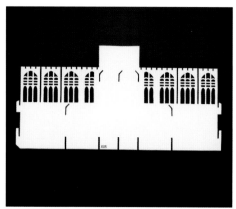

16. Cut out **X05** as shown in the figure.

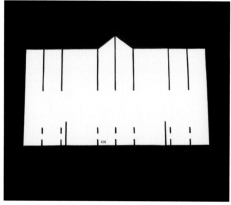

17. Cut out **X06** as shown in the figure.

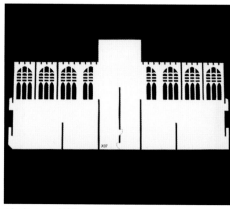

18. Cut out **X07** as shown in the figure.

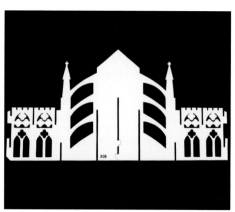

19. Cut out **X08** as shown in the figure.

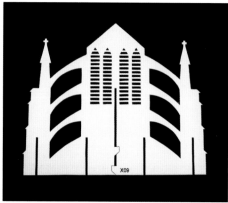

20. Cut out **X09** as shown in the figure.

21. Cut out **X10** as shown in the figure.

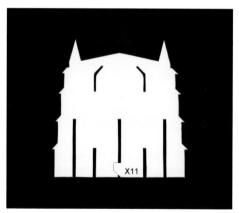

22. Cut out **X11** as shown in the figure.

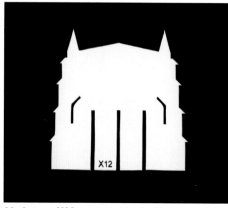

23. Cut out **X12** as shown in the figure.

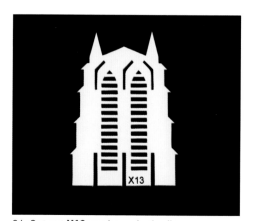

24. Cut out **X13** as shown in the figure.

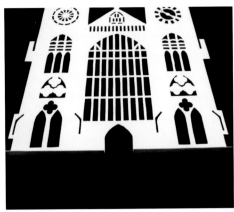

25. Fold **X01** as shown in the figure.

26. Interlock **X01** and **Y01** as shown in the figure.

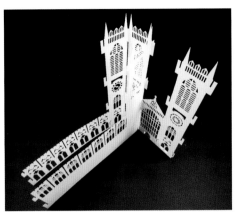

27. Interlock **Y03** to **X01** as shown in the figure.

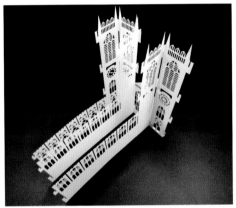

28. Interlock another **Y03** to **X01** as shown in the figure.

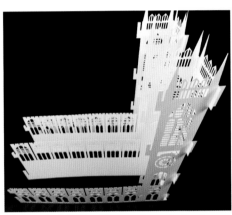

29. Interlock **Y02** to **X01** as shown in the figure.

30. Interlock **Y04** to **X02** as shown in the figure.

31. Interlock the unit from step 29 into the unit from step 30 as shown in the figure.

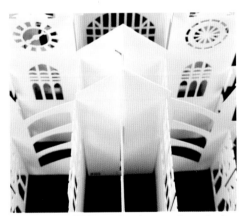

32. Interlock **X03** into the slots as shown in the figure.

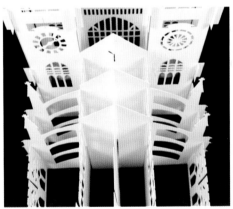

33. Interlock another **X03** into the slots as shown in the figure.

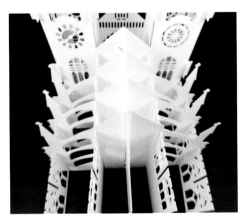

34. Interlock another **X03** into the slots as shown in the figure.

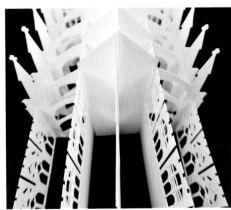

35. Interlock another **X03** into the slots as shown in the figure.

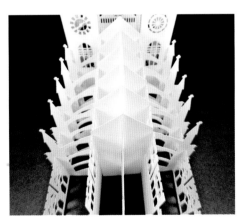

36. Interlock another **X03** into the slots as shown in the figure.

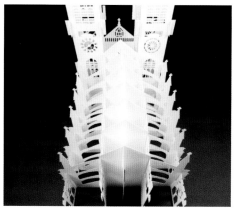

37. Interlock another **X03** into the slots as shown in the figure.

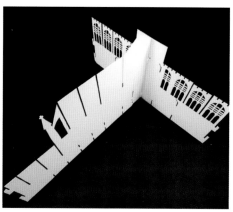

38. Interlock **Y05** into **X05** as shown in the figure.

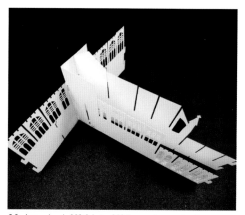

39. Interlock **Y06** into **X05** as shown in the figure.

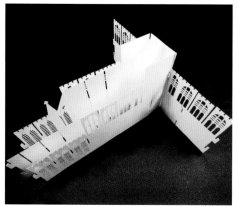

40. Interlock another **Y06** into **X05** as shown in the figure.

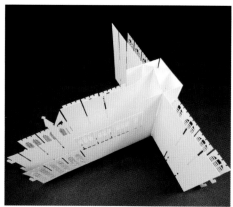

41. Interlock **X06** into the slots as shown in the figure.

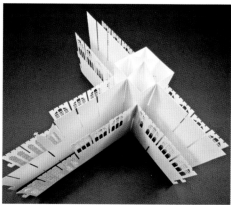

42. Interlock **X07** into the slots as shown in the figure.

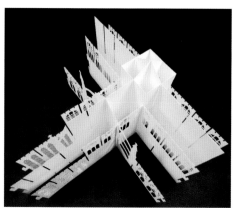

43. Interlock **X08** into the slots as shown in the figure.

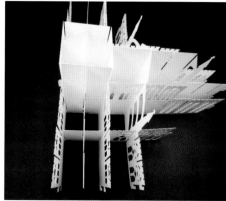

44. Interlock **Y07** into the slots as shown in the figure.

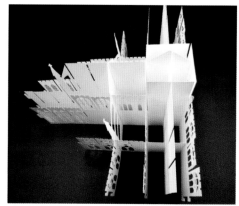

45. Rotate it 180 degrees. Interlock another **Y07** into the slots as shown in the figure.

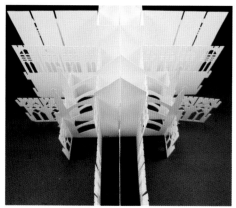

46. Interlock another **X03** into the slots as shown in the figure.

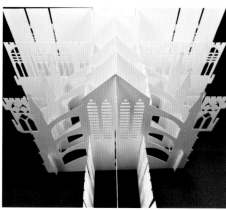

47. Interlock **X09** into the slots as shown in the figure.

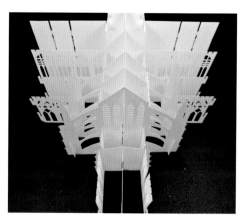

48. Interlock **X10** into the slots as shown in the figure.

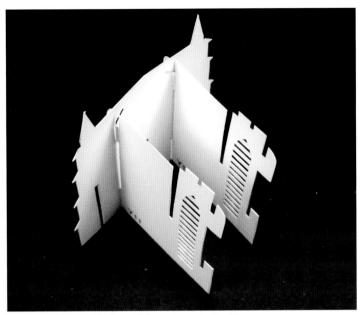

49, Interlock two **Y11** into **X11** as shown in the figure.

50. Interlock the unit into the slots as shown in the figure.

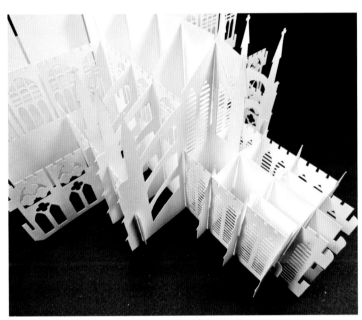

51. Interlock **X12** into the slots as shown in the figure.

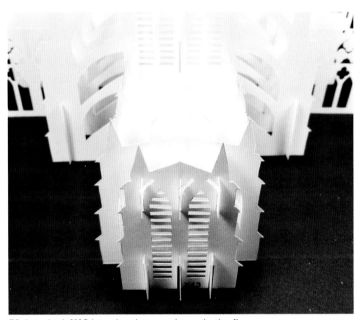

52. Interlock **X13** into the slots as shown in the figure.

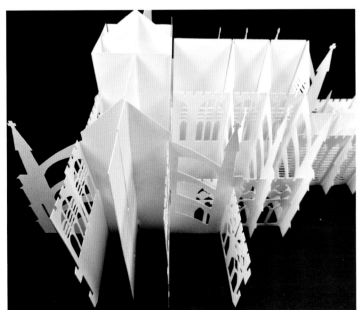

53. Interlock **Y08** into the slots as shown in the figure.

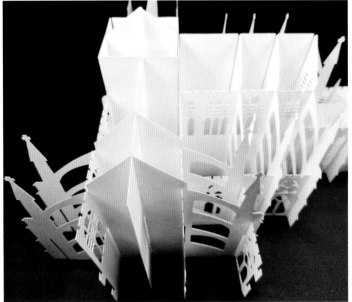

54. Interlock another **Y08** into the slots as shown in the figure.

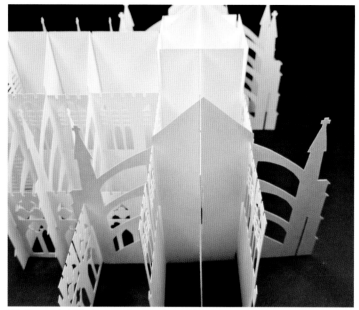

55. Rotate it 180 degree. Interlock another **Y08** into the slots as shown in the figure.

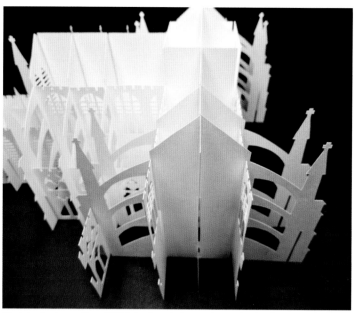

56. Interlock another **Y08** into the slots as shown in the figure.

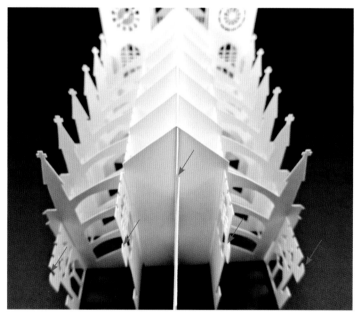

57. Interlock **X04** into the slots as shown in the figure.

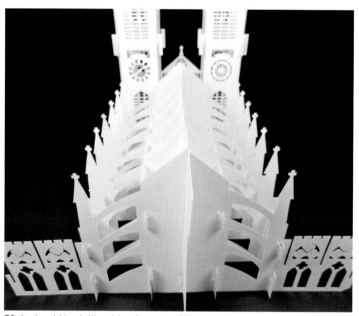

58. It should look like this after step 57 done.

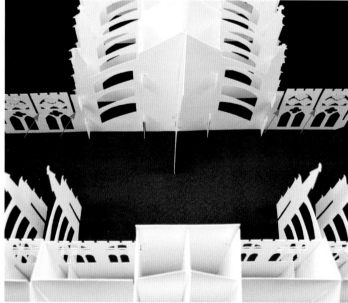

59. Interlock two units together as shown in the figure.

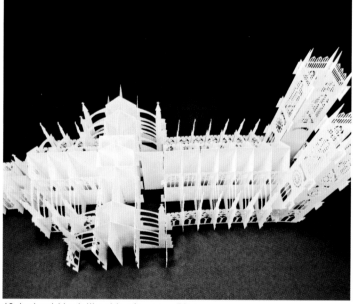

60. It should look like this after step 59 done.

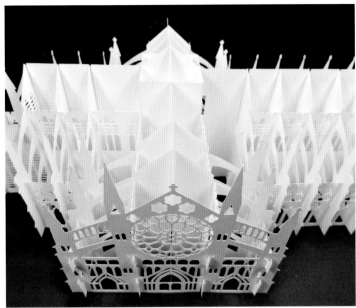

61. Interlock **Y10** into the slots as shown in the figure.

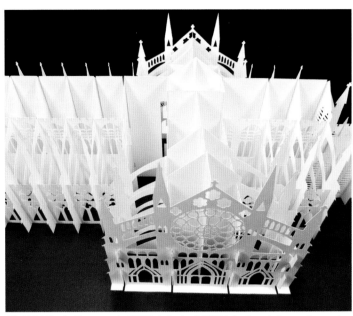

62. Fold the bottom part of **Y09**. Interlock **Y09** into the slots as shown in the figure.

63. Glue the folded parts of **X01** along the line as shown in the figure.

64. It should look like this after step 63 done.

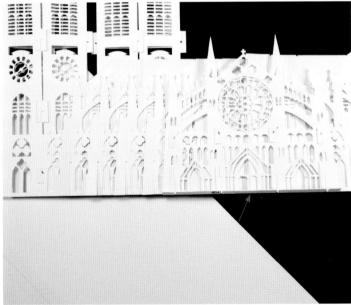

65. Fold down completely the building and apply glue on folded parts of **Y09** as shown in the figure.

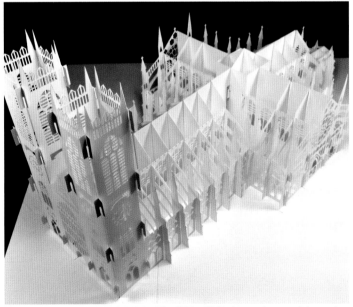

66. Close the baseboard tightly. The **Y09** will find a perfect position to be glued.

THE TOWER BRIDGE
London, England

Tower Bridge is the name of a combined bascule and suspension bridge in London, built across the River Thames and near the Tower of London, from which it got its name. It was designed by Horace Jones, the City Architect, in collaboration with John Wolfe Barry. The need for a new bridge became paramount in London, but due to heavy maritime traffic, the bridge would have to allow for ships to go up and down the river. Construction started in 1886, and it took eight years, five major contractors, and the labor of 432 construction workers to complete the Tower Bridge. The bridge was officially opened on 30 June 1894 by the Prince of Wales and his wife. A three-year restoration project was started in 2009 to refit and repaint this popular London landmark.

The Tower Bridge in terms of height, it stands tall at 213.2 feet or 65 meters. Its depth is measured at 60 feet or 18.3 meters, while its width is 800 feet or 243.8 meters.

Dimensions of the finished model:
(excluding the baseboard)
33.08 inches or 84.02 cm in length
4.84 inches or 12.3 cm in width
10.79 inches or 27.4 cm in height.

Pieces count: 54 pieces (excluding the baseboard)

Difficulty level: 7/10 (difficult)

Interlock pieces: Assemble the building without glue (excluding the baseboard).

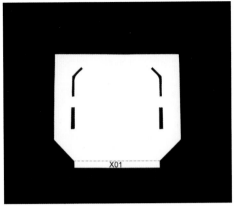

1. Cut out **X01** as shown in the figure. (2 pieces)

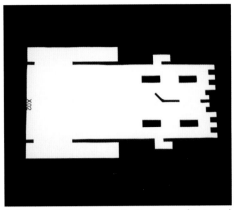

2. Cut out **X02** as shown in the figure. (4 pieces)

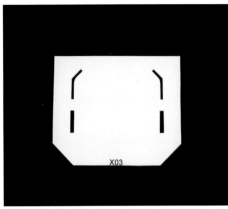

3. Cut out **X03** as shown in the figure. (2 pieces)

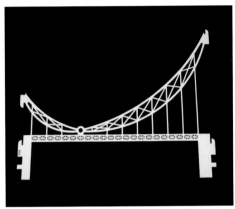

4. Cut out **X04** as shown in the figure. (4 pieces)

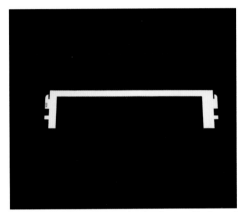

5. Cut out **X05** as shown in the figure. (5 pieces)

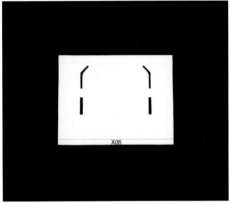

6. Cut out **X06** as shown in the figure. (2 pieces)

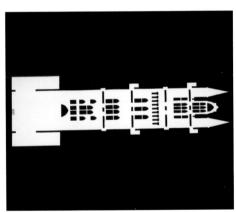

7. Cut out **X07** as shown in the figure. (4 pieces)

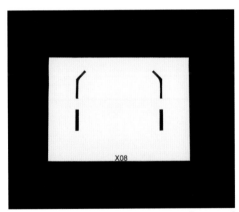

8. Cut out **X08** as shown in the figure. (2 pieces)

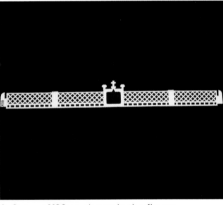

9. Cut out **X09** as shown in the figure

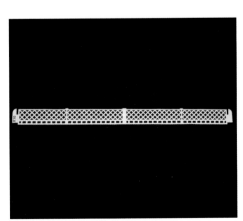

10. Cut out **X10** as shown in the figure. (3 pieces)

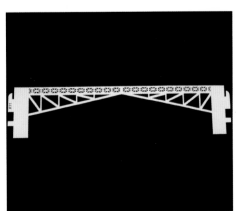

11. Cut out **X11** as shown in the figure. (2 pieces)

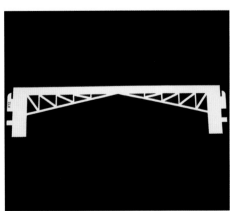

12. Cut out **X12** as shown in the figure. (3 pieces)

13. Cut out **X13** as shown in the figure. (4 pieces)

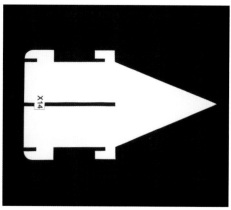

14. Cut out **X14** as shown in the figure. (4 pieces)

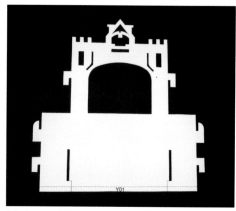

15. Cut out **Y01** as shown in the figure.

16. Cut out **Y02** as shown in the figure. (2 pieces)

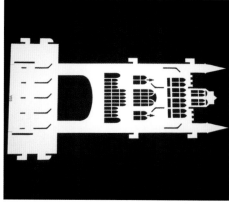

17. Cut out **Y03** as shown in the figure. (2 pieces)

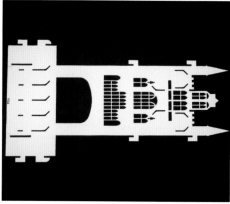

18. Cut out **Y04** as shown in the figure. (2 pieces)

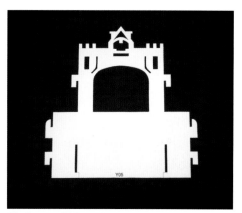

19. Cut out **Y05** as shown in the figure.

20. Cut out **Y06** as shown in the figure. (2 pieces)

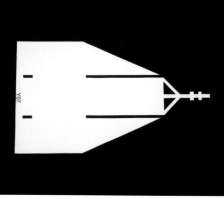

21. Cut out **Y07** as shown in the figure. (2 pieces)

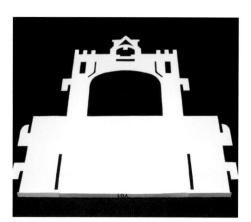

22. Fold **Y01** as shown in the figure.

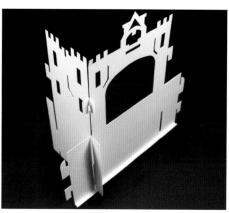

23. Interlock **X02** to **Y01** as shown in the figure.

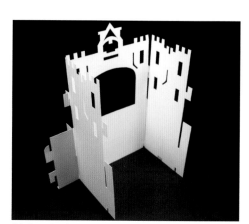

24. Interlock another **X02** to **Y01** as shown in the figure.

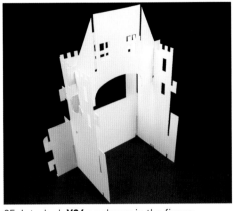

25. Interlock **Y06** as shown in the figure.

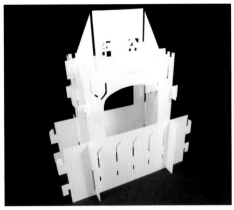

26. Interlock **Y02** as shown in the figure.

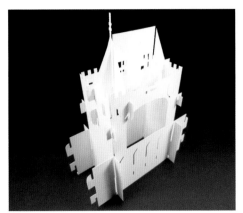

27. Interlock **X13** as shown in the figure.

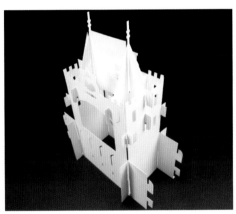

28. Interlock another **X13** as shown in the figure.

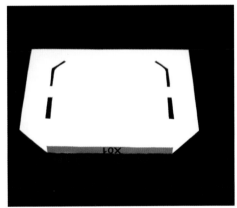

29. Fold **X01** as shown in the figure.

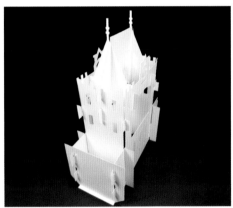

30. Interlock **X01** as shown in the figure.

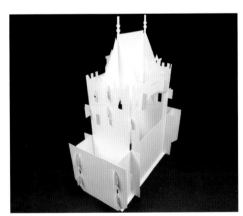

31. Rotate the unit 180 degree. Interlock **X03** as shown in the figure.

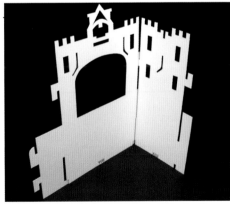

32. Interlock **X02** to **Y05** as shown in the figure.

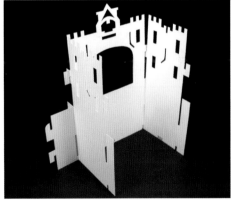

33. Interlock another **X02** to **Y05** as shown in the figure.

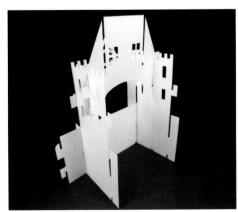

34. Interlock **Y06** as shown in the figure.

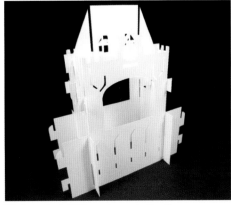

35. Interlock **Y02** as shown in the figure.

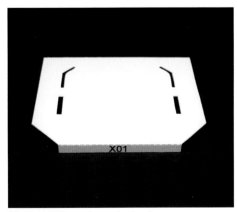

36. Fold **X01** as shown in the figure.

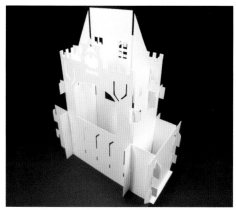

37. Interlock **X01** as shown in the figure.

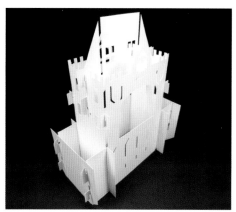

38. Interlock **X03** as shown in the figure.

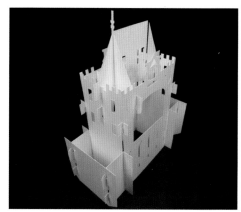

39. Interlock **X13** as shown in the figure.

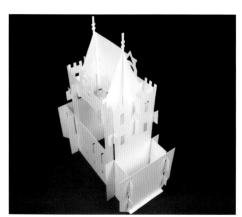

40. Interlock **X13** as shown in the figure.

41. Interlock **X14** to **Y03** and **Y04** as shown in the figure.

42. It should look like this after step 41 done.

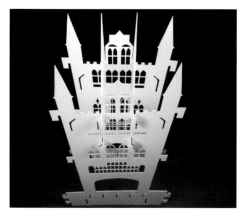

43. Interlock **X14** as shown in the figure.

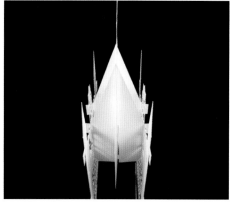

44. Slide **Y07** from bottom to Interlock into both **X14** as shown in the figure.

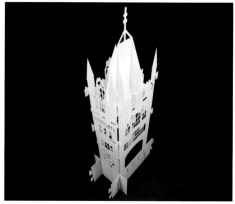

45. Interlock **X07** as shown in the figure.

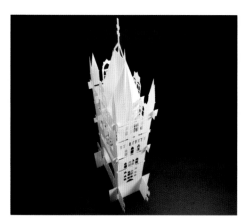

46. Rotate the unit 180 degrees. Interlock **X07** as shown in the figure.

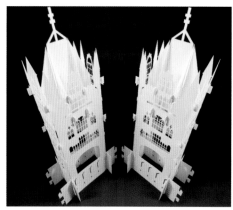

47. Repeat step 41 to 46 to make two components total.

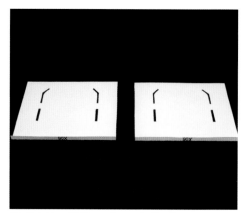

48. Fold two **X06** as shown in the figure.

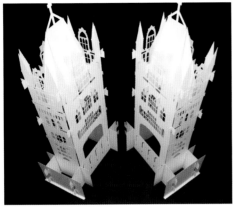

49. Interlock two **X06** into the units as shown in the figure.

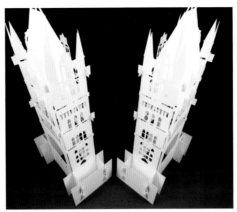

50. Rotate each unit 180 degrees. Interlock **X08** into each unit as shown in the figure.

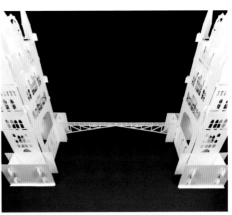

51. Interlock **X11** into both units as shown in the figure.

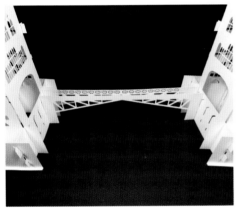

52. Interlock **X12** into both units as shown in the figure.

53. Interlock another **X12** into both units as shown in the figure.

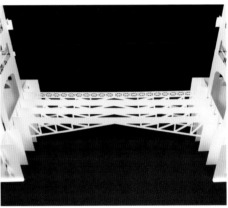

54. Interlock another **X12** into both units as shown in the figure.

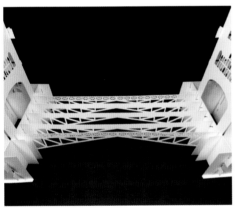

55. Interlock **X11** into both units as shown in the figure.

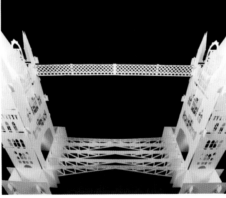

56. Interlock **X10** into both units as shown in the figure.

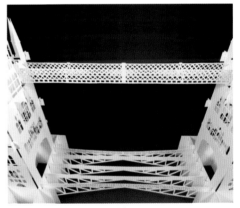

57. Interlock another **X10** into both units as shown in the figure.

58. Interlock another **X10** into both units as shown in the figure.

59. Interlock **X09** into both units as shown in the figure.

60. Interlock **X04** into both units as shown in the figure.

61. Interlock **X05** into both units as shown in the figure.

62. Interlock another **X05** into both units as shown in the figure.

63. Interlock another **X05** into both units as shown in the figure.

64. Interlock **X04** into both units as shown in the figure.

65. On the other side, interlock **X04** into both units as shown in the figure.

66. Interlock **X05** into both units as shown in the figure.(

67. Interlock another **X05** into both units as shown in the figure.

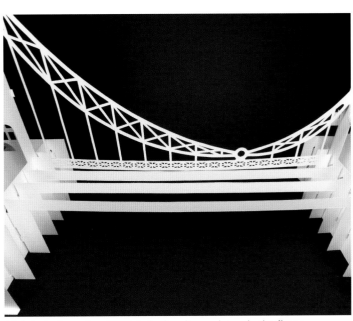

68. Interlock another **X05** into both units as shown in the figure.

69. Interlock **X04** into both units as shown in the figure.

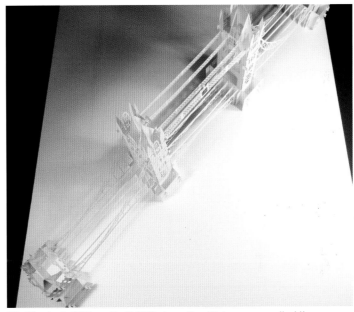

70. Glue both **X01** and both **X06** along the 45 degree penciled line as shown in the figure. Erase remain penciled lines.

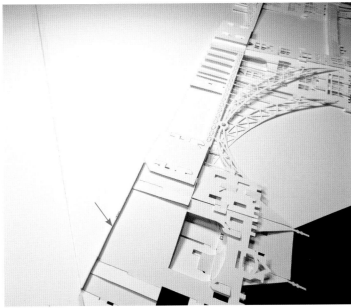

71. Fold down the building completely and apply glue on folded parts of **Y01** as shown in the figure.

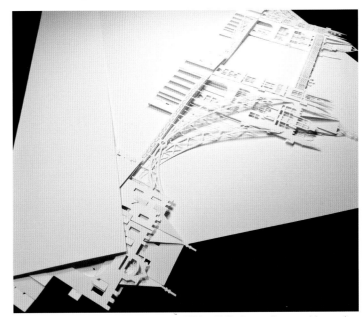

72. Close the baseboard tightly. The **Y01** will find a perfect position to be glued.

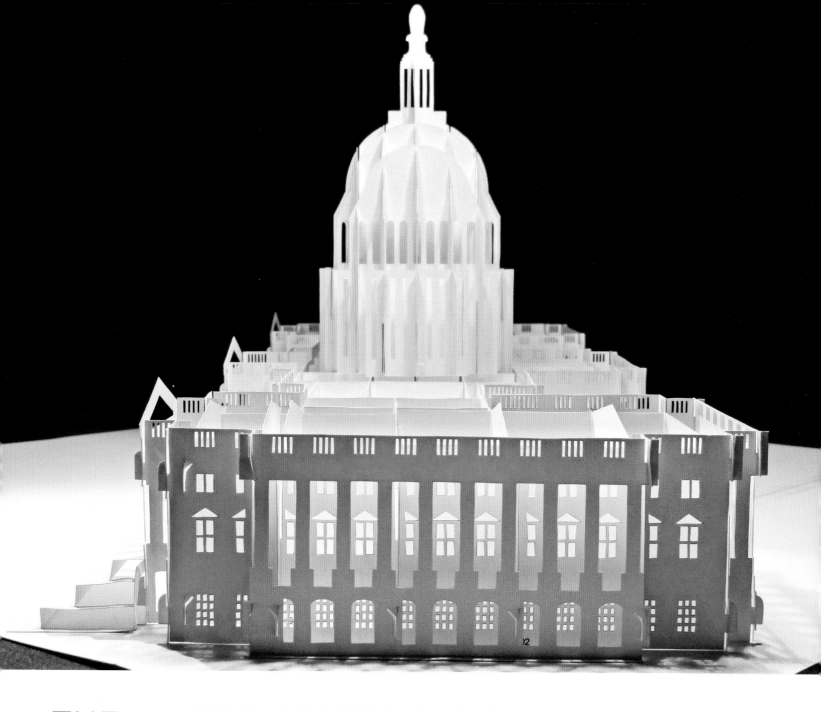

THE UNITED STATES CAPITOL BUILDING
Washington D.C., USA

The United States Capitol Building, the meeting chambers for the Senate and the House of Representatives, is one of the most recognizable historic buildings in Washington, DC, located at the opposite end of the National Mall from the Washington Monument. It is a prominent landmark and an impressive example of 19th-century neoclassical architecture. Begun in 1793, the Capitol has been built, burnt, rebuilt, extended, and restored; today, it stands as a monument not only to its builders but also to the American people and their government. As the twenty-first century opens, the Capitol complex is still growing and changing.

United States Capitol in terms of height, it stands tall at 288 feet or 87.8 meters. Its depth is measured at 350 feet or 106.7 meters, while its width is 751 feet or 229 meters.

Dimensions of the finished model:
(excluding the baseboard)
22.16 inches or 56.3 cm in length
7.11 inches or 18.1 cm in width
8.57 inches or 21.8 cm in height.

Pieces count: 71 pieces (excluding the baseboard)

Difficulty level: 8/10 (very hard)

Interlock pieces: Assemble the building without glue (excluding the baseboard).

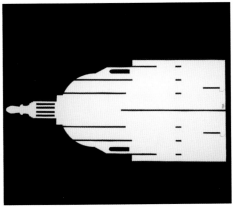

1. Cut out **T01** as shown in the figure.

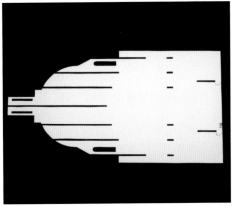

2. Cut out **T02** as shown in the figure.

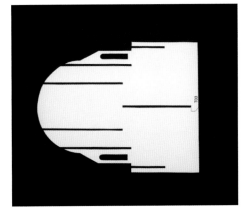

3. Cut out **T03** as shown in the figure. (2 pieces)

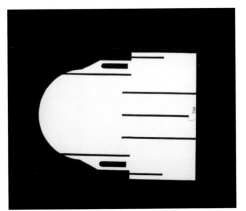

4. Cut out **T04** as shown in the figure. (2 pieces)

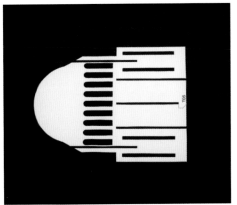

5. Cut out **T05** as shown in the figure. (2 pieces)

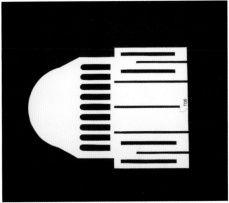

6. Cut out **T06** as shown in the figure. (2 pieces)

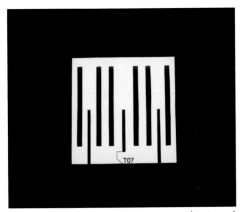

7. Cut out **T07** as shown in the figure. (4 pieces)

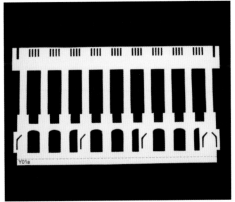

8. Cut out **Y01a** as shown in the figure.

9. Cut out **Y02** as shown in the figure. (2 pieces)

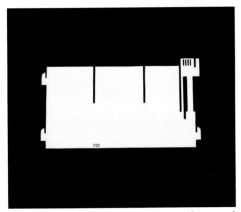

10. Cut out **Y03** as shown in the figure. (4 pieces)

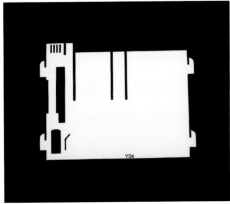

11. Cut out **Y04** as shown in the figure. (4 pieces)

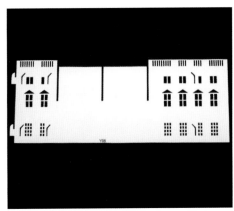

12. Cut out **Y05** as shown in the figure. (2 pieces)

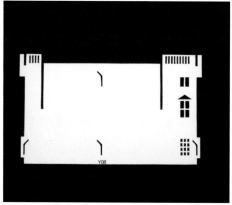

13. Cut out **Y06** as shown in the figure. (2 pieces)

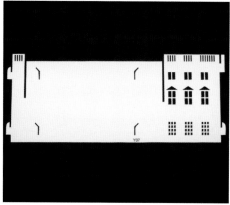

14. Cut out **Y07** as shown in the figure. (2 pieces)

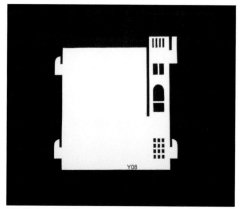

15. Cut out **Y08** as shown in the figure. (2 pieces)

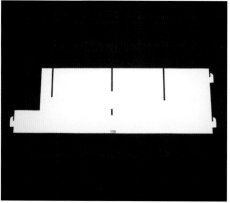

16. Cut out **Y09** as shown in the figure. (2 pieces)

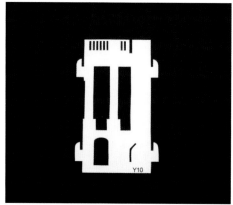

17. Cut out **Y10** as shown in the figure. (2 pieces)

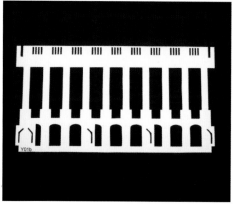

18. Cut out **Y01b** as shown in the figure.

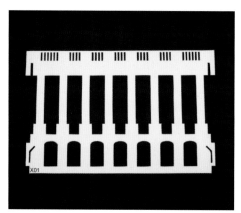

19. Cut out **X01** as shown in the figure. (2 pieces)

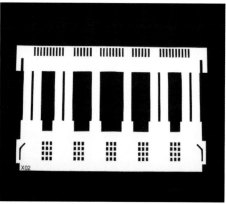

20. Cut out **X02** as shown in the figure.

21. Cut out **X03** as shown in the figure. (2 pieces)

22. Cut out **X04** as shown in the figure.

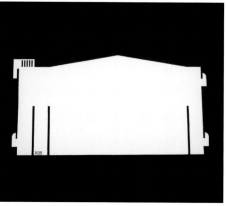

23. Cut out **X05** as shown in the figure. (2 pieces)

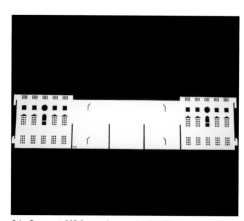

24. Cut out **X06** as shown in the figure.

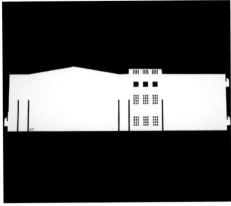

25. Cut out **X07** as shown in the figure. (2 pieces)

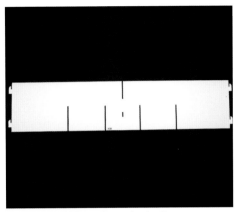

26. Cut out **X08** as shown in the figure. (2 pieces)

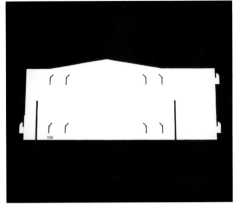

27. Cut out **X09** as shown in the figure. (2 pieces)

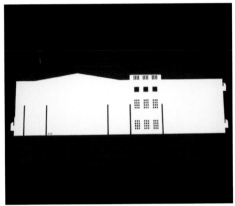

28. Cut out **X10** as shown in the figure. (2 pieces)

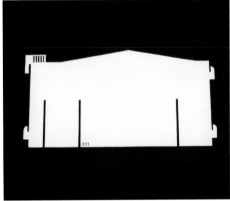

29. Cut out **X11** as shown in the figure. (2 pieces)

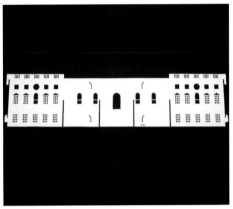

30. Cut out **X12** as shown in the figure.

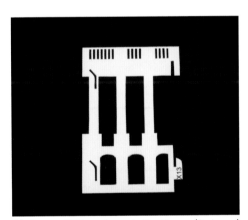

31. Cut out **X13** as shown in the figure. (2 pieces)

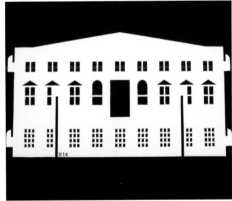

32. Cut out **X14** as shown in the figure. (2 pieces)

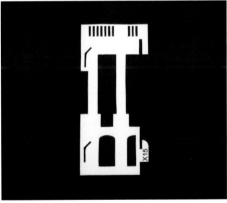

33. Cut out **X15** as shown in the figure. (4 pieces)

34. Cut out **X16** as shown in the figure.

35. Cut out **X17** as shown in the figure. (2 pieces)

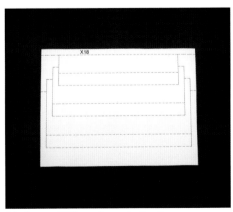

36. Cut out **X18** as shown in the figure.

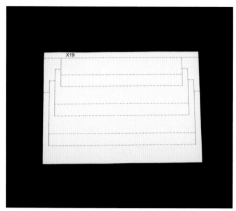

37. Cut out **X19** as shown in the figure. (2 pieces)

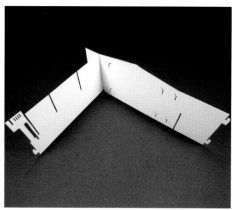

38. Interlock **X09** and **Y03** together as shown in the figure.

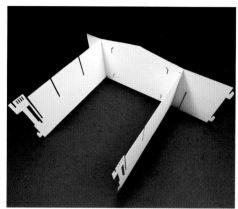

39. Interlock another **Y03** into **X09** as shown in the figure.

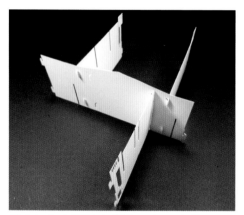

40. Interlock **Y04** into **X09** as shown in the figure.

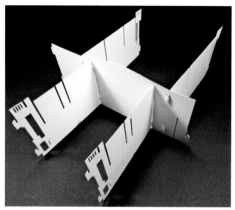

41. Interlock another **Y04** into **X09** as shown in the figure.

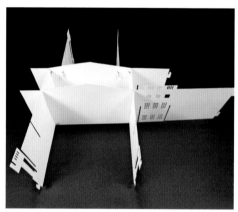

42. Interlock **X07** into the slots as shown in the figure.

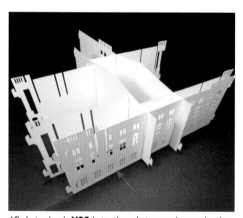

43. Interlock **Y02** into the slots as shown in the figure.

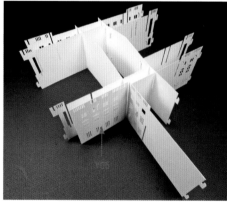

44. Interlock **Y05** into the slots as shown in the figure.

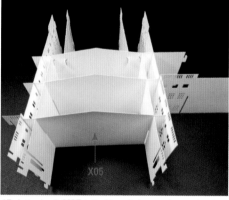

45. Interlock **X05** into the slots as shown in the figure.

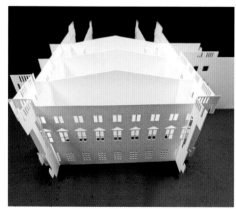

46. Interlock **X03** into the slots as shown in the figure.

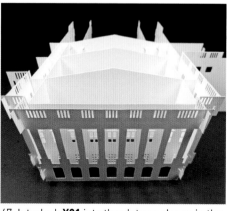

47. Interlock **X01** into the slots as shown in the figure.

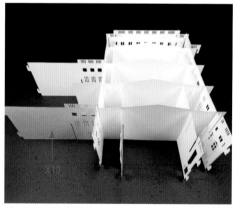

48. Interlock **X10** into the slots as shown in the figure.

49. Interlock **X11** into the slots as shown in the figure.

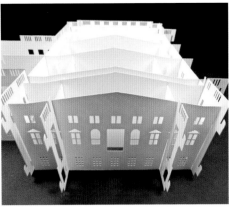

50. Interlock **X14** into the slots as shown in the figure.

51. Interlock **X15** into the slots as shown in the figure.

52. Interlock another **X15** into the slots as shown in the figure.

53. Fold the lower part of **X17** as shown in the figure.

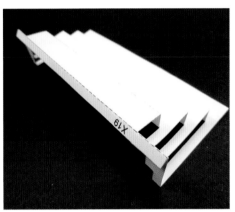

54. Fold **X19** as shown in the figure.

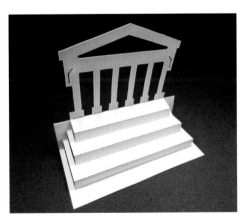

55. Apply glue to join **X17** and **X19** as shown in the figure.

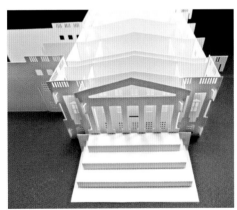

56. Interlock the unit into the slots as shown in the figure.

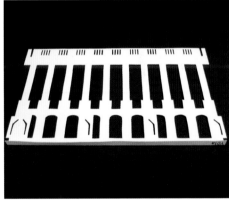

57. Fold the lower part of **Y01a** as shown in the figure.

58. Interlock **Y01a** into the slots as shown in the figure.

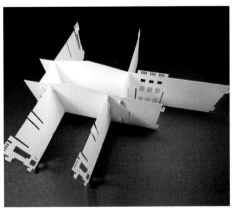

59. Interlock **X07, X09**, two **Y03** and two **Y04** together as shown in the figure.

60. Interlock **Y05** into the slots as shown in the figure.

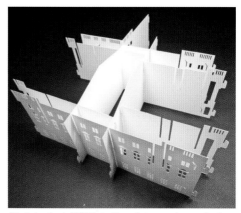

61. Interlock **Y02** into the slots as shown in the figure.

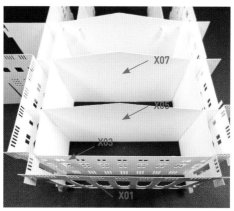

62. Interlock **X01, X03, X05** and **X07** into the slots as shown in the figure.

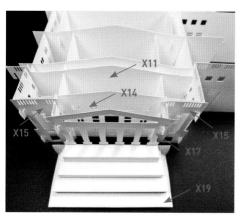

63. Fold and glue **X17** and **X19**. Interlock **X11**, **X14**, **X17** and two **X15** into the slots as shown in the figure.

64. Interlock **Y01b** into the slots as shown in the figure.

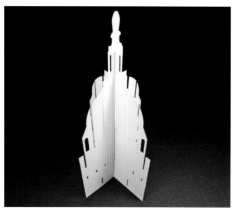

65. Interlock **T01** and **T02** together as shown in the figure.

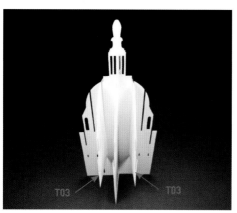

66. Interlock two **T03** into **T01** as shown in the figure.

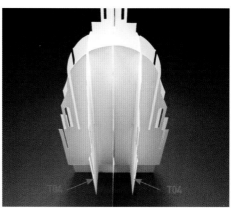

67. Interlock two **T04** into the slots as shown in the figure.

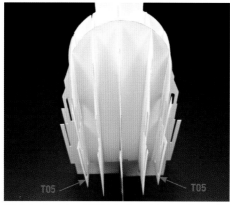

68. Interlock two **T05** into the slots as shown in the figure.

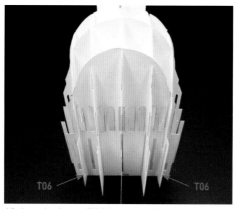

69. Interlock two **T06** into the slots as shown in the figure.

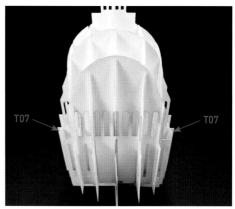

70. Interlock two **T07** into the slots as shown in the figure.

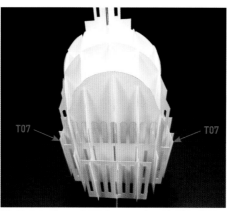

71. Rotate the unit 90 degrees Interlock other two **T07** into the slots as shown in the figure.

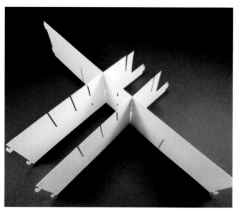

72. Interlock two **Y09** into **X08** as shown in the figure.

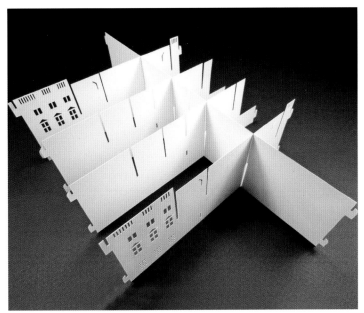

73. Interlock two **Y07** into **X08** as shown in the figure.

74. Interlock another **X08** into the slots as shown in the figure.

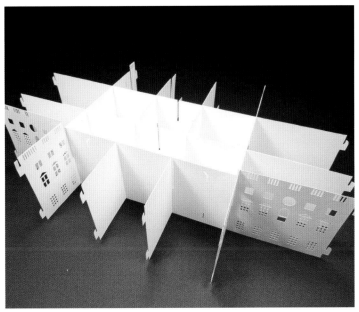

75. Interlock **X06** into the slots as shown in the figure.

76. Interlock two **Y08** into **X06** as shown in the figure.

77. Interlock **X04** into the slots as shown in the figure.

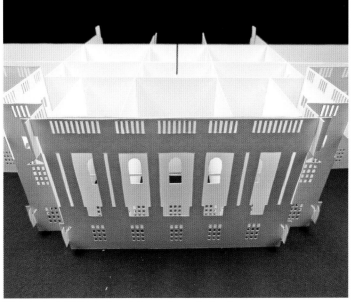

78. Interlock **X02** into the slots as shown in the figure.

79. Rotate the unit 90 degrees. Interlock **Y06** into the slots as shown in the figure.

80. Rotate the unit 180 degrees. Interlock **Y06** into the slots as shown in the figure.

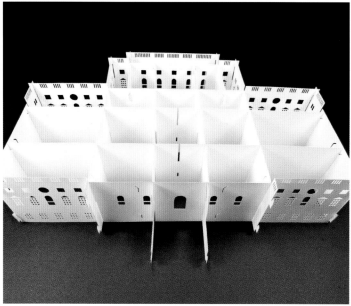

81. Interlock **X12** into the slots as shown in the figure.

82. Interlock **Y10** into **X12** as shown in the figure.

83. Interlock another **Y10** into **X12** as shown in the figure.

84. Interlock **X13** into the slots as shown in the figure.

85. Interlock another **X13** into the slots as shown in the figure.

86. Fold **X16** as shown in the figure.

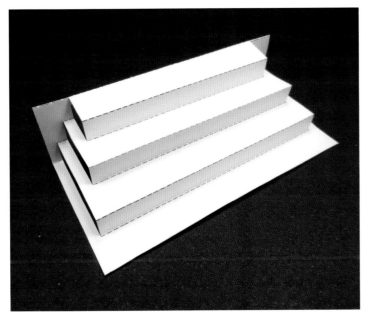

87. Fold **X18** as shown in the figure. Apply glue on the folded edge to join **X16** together.

88. It should look like this after step 87 done.

89. Interlock it into the unit from step 85 as shown in the figure.

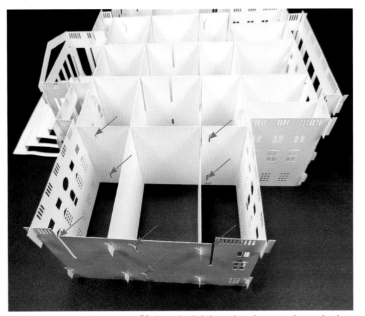

90. Take the unit from step 58. Interlock it into the slots as shown in the figure.

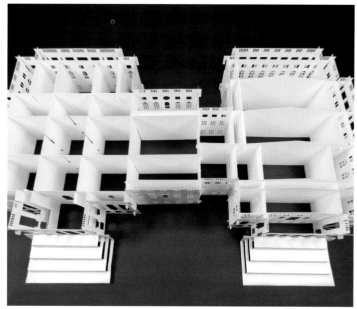

91. It should look like this after step 90 done.

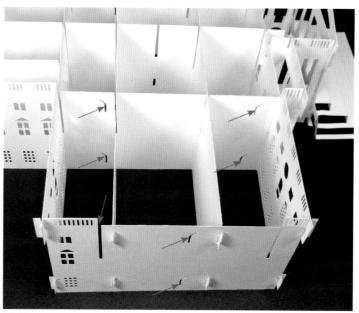

92. Take the unit from step 64. Interlock it into the slots as shown in the figure.

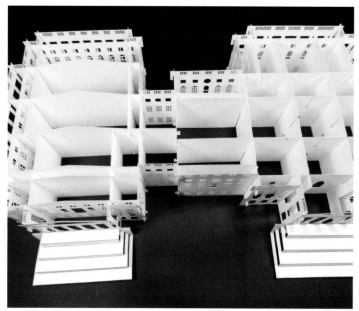

93. It should look like this after step 92 done.

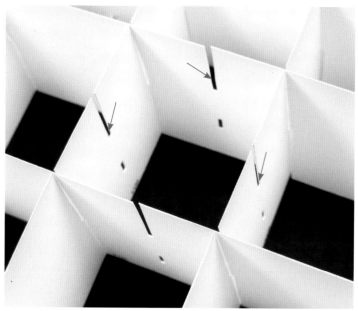

94. Take the unit from step 71. Interlock it into the slots as shown in the figure.

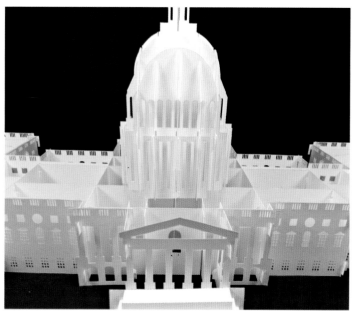

95. It should look like this after step 94 done.

96. Glue **Y01a** along the 45 degrees penciled line as shown in the figure.

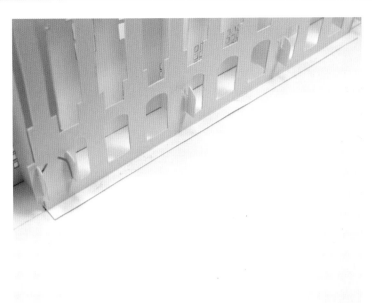

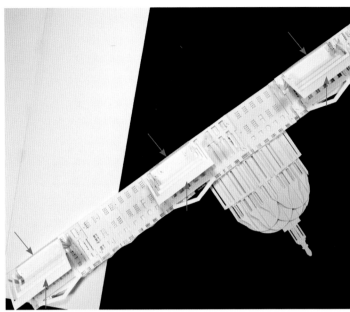

97. It should look like this after step 96 done. Erase remain penciled lines.

98. Fold down the building completely and apply glue on folded edges of **X16**, two **X17, X18** and two **X19** as shown in the figure.

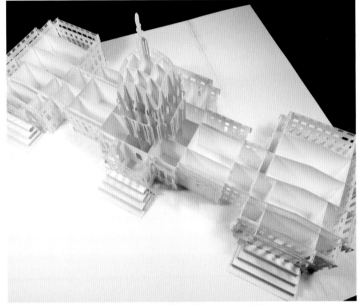

99. Close the baseboard tightly. All folded edges will find a perfect position to be glued by themselves.

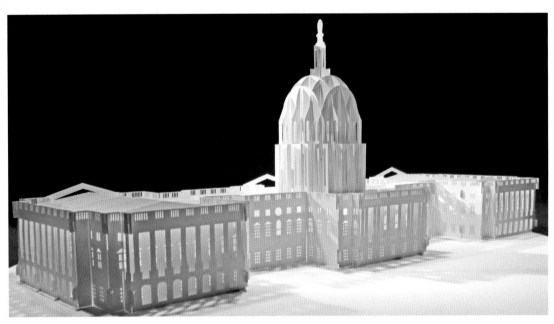

THE CHRYSLER BUILDING
New York City, USA

The Chrysler Building, once the world's tallest structure, also was one of the most attractive office buildings in the world. This was one of the first large buildings with extensive metalwork and has 3,862 windows on its façade. Architect William Van Alen designed the building for Walter P. Chrysler, as part of an intense competition to build the world's tallest skyscraper. Construction began on September 19, 1928 and was completed by May 28, 1930, only nine months! The building was meant to be the headquarters of the Chrysler Corporation, hence the car hood ornament replicas found near the top of the building. The highest occupied floor in the building is the 71st floor, above that level the remaining floors are designed only for exterior beautification.

The Chrysler Building in New York City, located on the east side of Manhattan in the Turtle Bay area. In terms of height, it stands tall at 1047 feet or 319 meters.

Dimensions of the finished model:
(excluding the baseboard)
6.05 inches or 15.3 cm in length
6.05 inches or 15.3 cm in width
27.37 inches or 69.5 cm in height.

Pieces count: 213 pieces (excluding the baseboard)

Difficulty level: 8/10 (very hard)

1. Cut out **X01** as shown in the figure. (2 pieces)

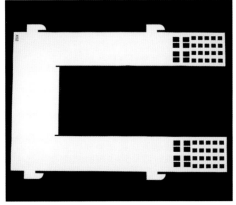

2. Cut out **X02** as shown in the figure. (2 pieces)

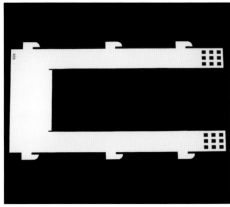

3. Cut out **X03** as shown in the figure. (2 pieces)

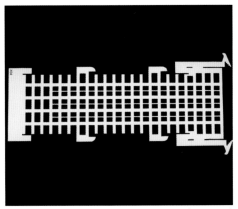

4. Cut out **X04** as shown in the figure. (2 pieces)

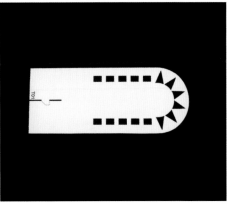

5. Cut out **X05** as shown in the figure. (2 pieces)

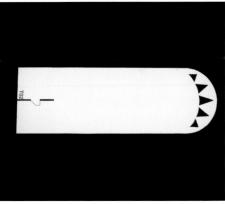

6. Cut out **X06** as shown in the figure. (2 pieces)

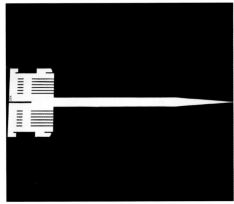

7. Cut out **X07** as shown in the figure.

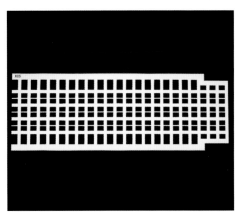

8. Cut out **T01** as shown in the figure. (4 pieces)

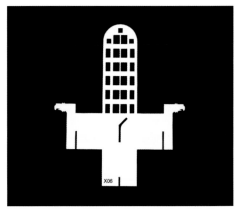

9. Cut out **T02** as shown in the figure. (4 pieces)

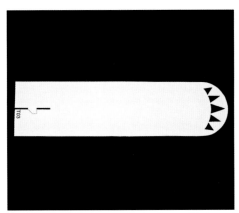

10. Cut out **T03** as shown in the figure. (4 pieces)

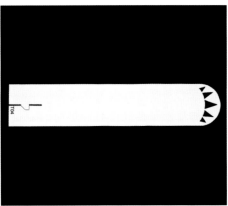

11. Cut out **T04** as shown in the figure. (4 pieces)

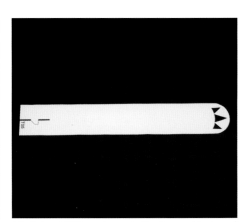

12. Cut out **T05** as shown in the figure. (4 pieces)

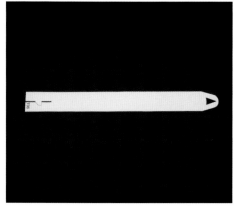

13. Cut out **T06** as shown in the figure. (4 pieces)

14. Cut out **Y01** as shown in the figure. (2 pieces)

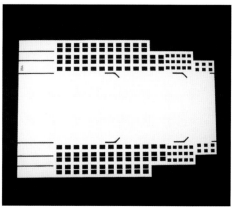

15. Cut out **Y02** as shown in the figure. (2 pieces)

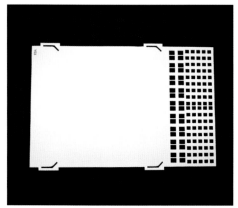

16. Cut out **Y03** as shown in the figure. (2 pieces)

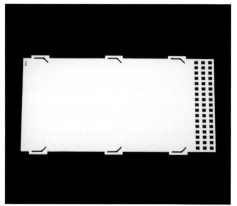

17. Cut out **Y04** as shown in the figure. (2 pieces)

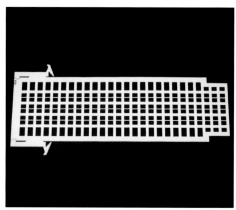

18. Cut out **Y05** as shown in the figure. (2 pieces)

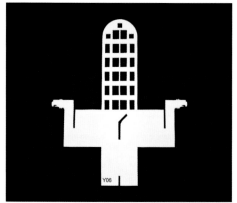

19. Cut out **Y06** as shown in the figure. (2 pieces)

20. Cut out **Y07** as shown in the figure. (2 pieces)

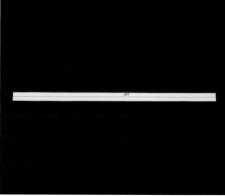

21. Cut out **J01** as shown in the figure. (2 pieces)

22. Cut out **J02** as shown in the figure. (160 pieces)

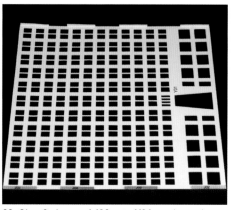

23. Glue 8 pieces of **J02** onto **Y01** as shown in the figure.

24. Glue **X01** and **Y01** together with **J02** as shown in the figure.

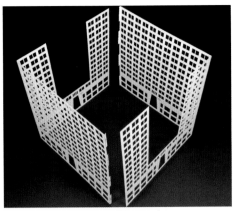

25. Repeat step 23 and 24 to make two components total. Glue two components together with **J02** as shown in the figure.

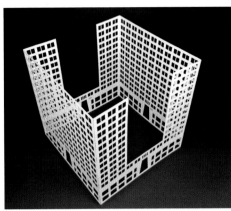

26. It should look like this after step 25 done. Interlock **Y03** into the slots as shown in the figure.

27. Glue a **J01** to the bottom of **X01** and another **J01** to the bottom of **Y01** as shown in the figure.

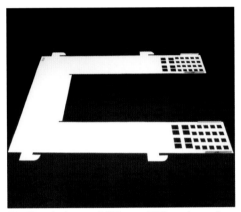

28. Glue 4 pieces of **J02** onto **X02** as shown in the figure.

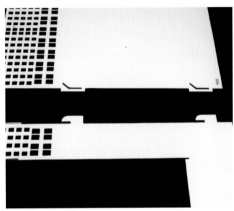

29. Interlock and glue **X02** and **Y03** as shown in the figure.

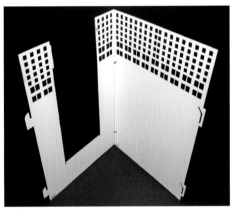

30. It should look like this after step 29 done.

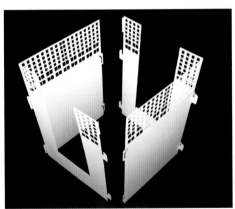

31. Repeat step 28 and 29 to make two components total. Interlock and glue two components together as shown in the figure.

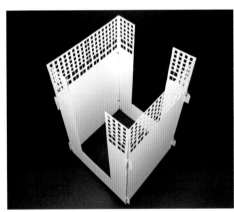

32. It should look like this after step 31 done.

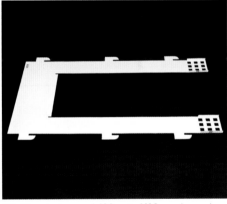

33. Glue 4 pieces of **J02** onto **X03** as shown in the figure.

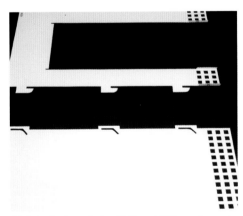

34. Interlock and glue **X03** and **Y04** as shown in the figure.

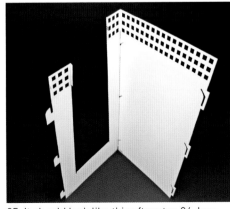

35. It should look like this after step 34 done.

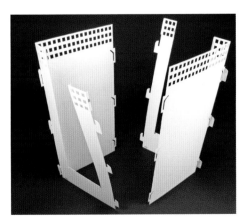

36. Repeat step 33 and 34 to make two components total. Interlock and glue two components together as shown in the figure.

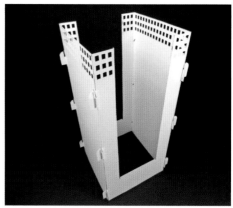

37. It should look like this after step 36 done.

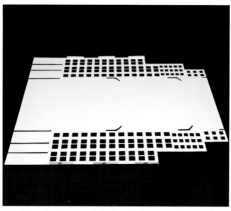

38. Glue 6 pieces of **J02** onto **Y02** as shown in the figure.

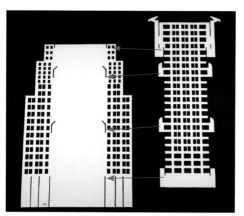

39. Interlock **X04** and **Y02** as shown in the figure.

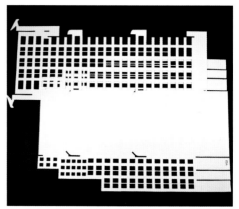

40. It should look like this after step 39 done.

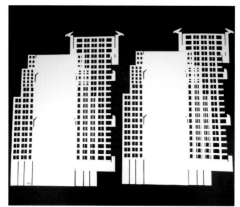

41. Repeat step 38 and 39 to make two components total

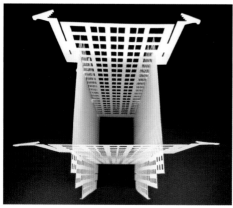

42. Interlock two components together as shown in the figure.

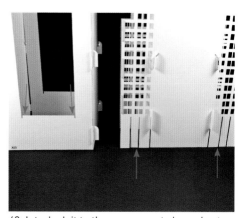

43. Interlock it to the component shown in step 37 as shown in the figure.

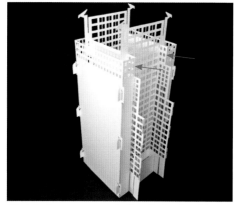

44. Join four upper parts (two in the front two in the back) with glue as shown in the figure.

45. Interlock it to the component in step 32 as shown in the figure.

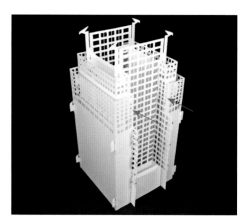

46. Join four upper parts (two in the front two in the back) with glue as shown in the figure.

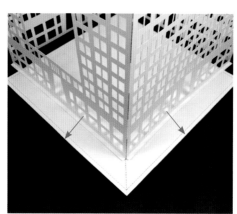

47. Glue the two J01 in the component shown in step 26 to the baseboard as shown in the figure.

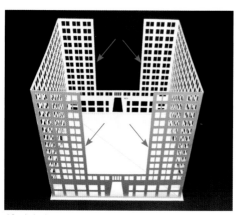

48. Join it to the component shown in step 46 with glue.

49. It should look like this after step 48 done.

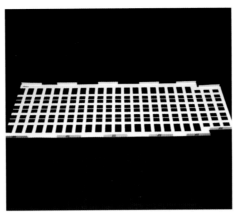

50. Glue 12 pieces of **J02** onto **X05** as shown in the figure.

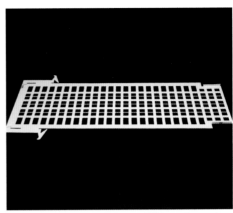

51. Glue 2 pieces of **J02** onto **Y05** as shown in the figure.

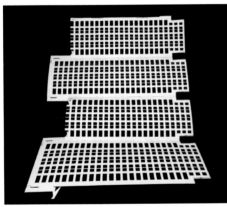

52. Join **X05** and **Y05** together as shown in the figure.

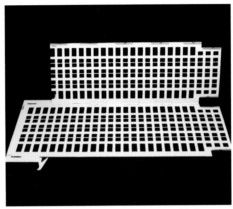

53. It should look like this after step 52 done.

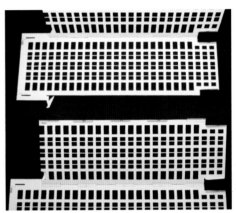

54. Repeat step 50 to 52 to make two components total. Join two components together as shown in the figure.

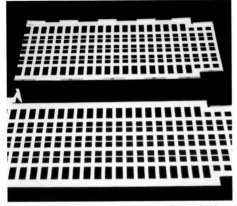

55. Join two sides together as shown in the figure.

56. It should look like this after step 55 done.

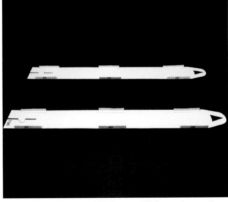

57. Glue 6 pieces of **J02** onto **T06** as shown in the figure. Make two sets.

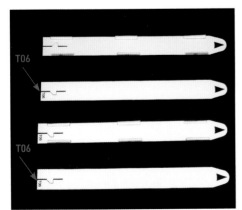

58. Add two pieces of **T06** as shown in the figure. Join them together as shown in the figure.

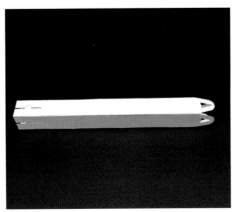

59. It should look like this after step 58 done.

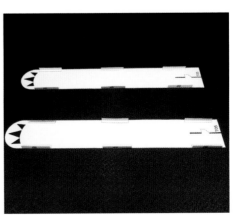

60. Glue 6 pieces of **J02** onto **T05** as shown in the figure. Make two sets.

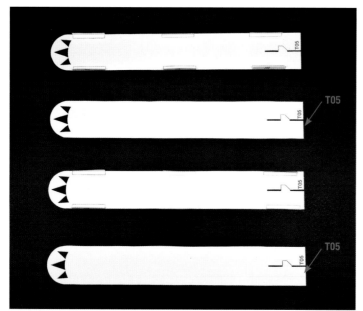

61. Add two pieces of **T05** as shown in the figure. Join them together as shown in the figure.

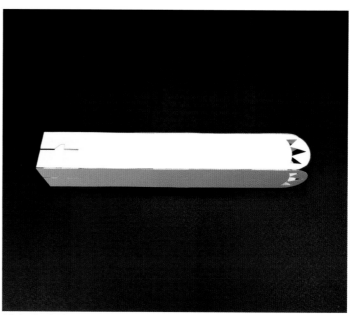

62. It should look like this after step 61 done.

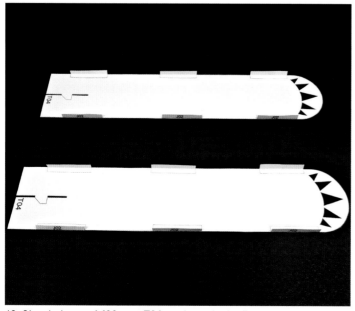

63. Glue 6 pieces of **J02** onto **T04** as shown in the figure. Make two sets.

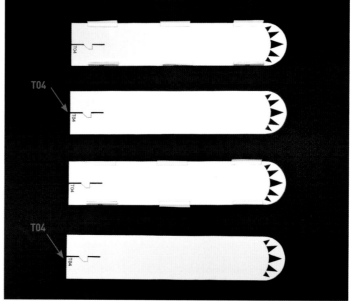

64. Add two pieces of **T04** as shown in the figure. Join them together as shown in the figure.

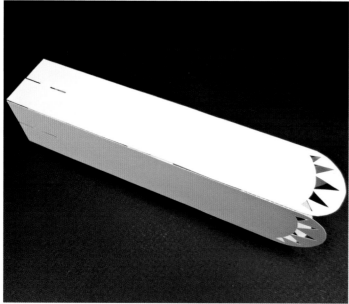

65. It should look like this after step 64 done.

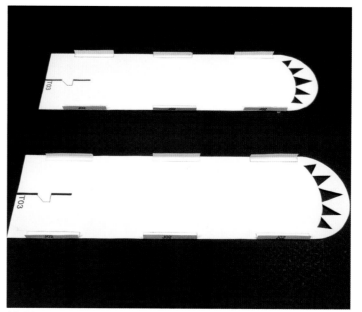

66. Glue 6 pieces of **J02** onto **T03** as shown in the figure. Make two sets.

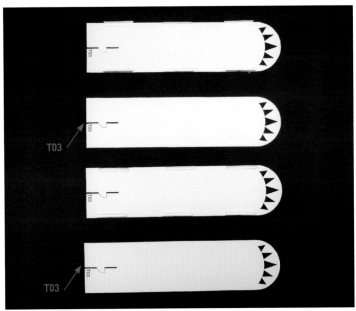

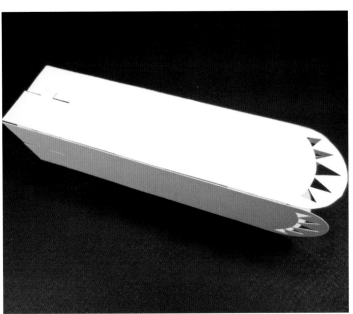

67. Add two pieces of **T03** as shown in the figure. Join them together as shown in the figure.

68. It should look like this after step 67 done.

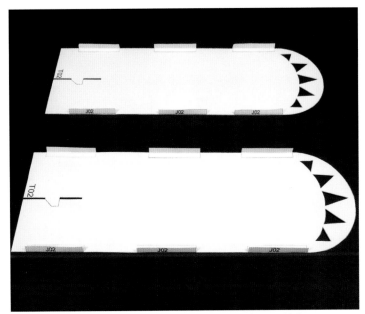

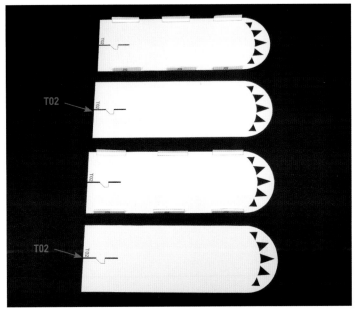

69. Glue 6 pieces of **J02** onto **T03** as shown in the figure. Make two sets.

70. Add two pieces of **T02** as shown in the figure. Join them together as shown in the figure.

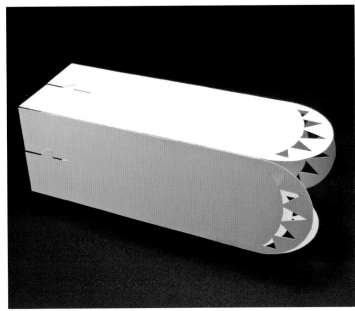

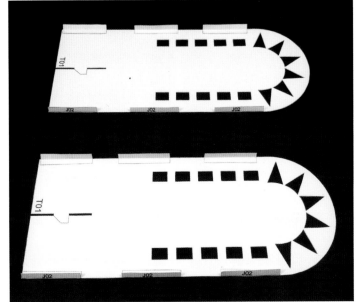

71. It should look like this after step 70 done.

72. Glue 6 pieces of **J02** onto **T01** as shown in the figure. Make two sets.

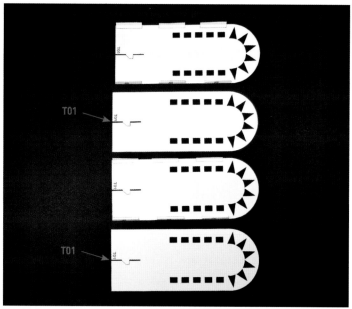

73. Add two pieces of **T01** as shown in the figure. Join them together as shown in the figure.

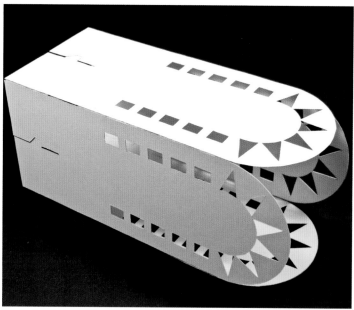

74. It should look like this after step 73 done.

75. Interlock **X07** and **Y07** together as shown in the figure.

76. Interlock it to the component shown in step 59 as shown in the figure.

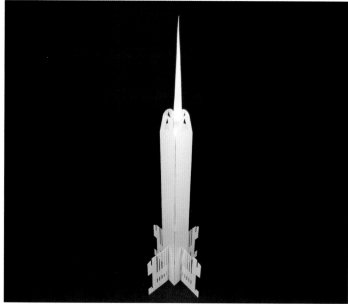

77. It should look like this after step 76 done.

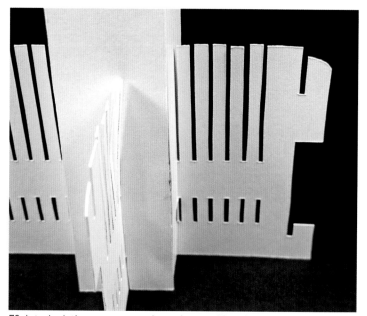

78. Interlock the component shown in step 62 to the slots next to the slots just used as shown in the figure.

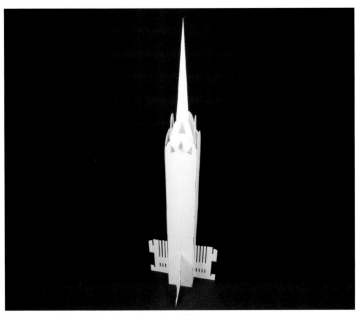

79. It should look like this after step 78 done.

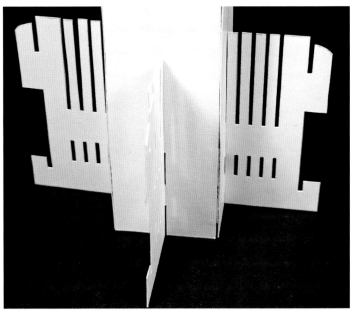

80. Interlock the component shown in step 65 to the slots next to the slots just used as shown in the figure.

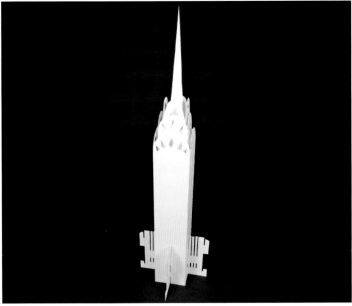

81. It should look like this after step 80 done.

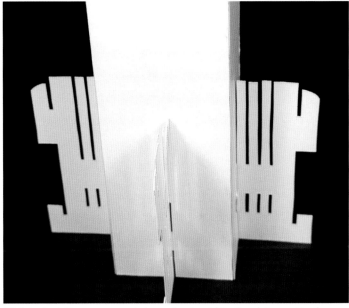

82. Interlock the component shown in step 68 to the slots next to the slots just used as shown in the figure.

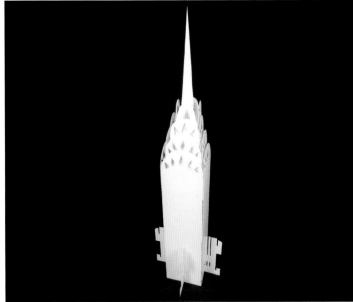

83. It should look like this after step 82 done.

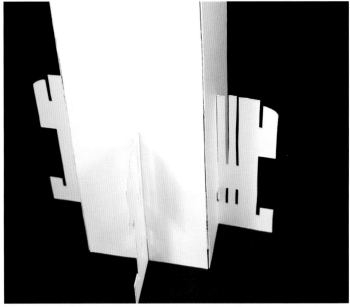

84. Interlock the component shown in step 71 to the slots next to the slots just used as shown in the figure.

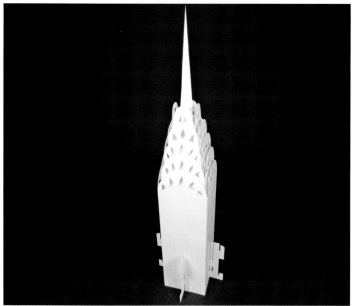

85. It should look like this after step 84 done.

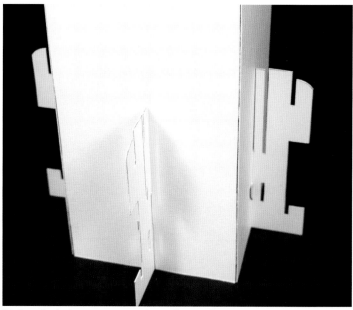

86. Interlock the component shown in step 74 to the slots next to the slots just used as shown in the figure.

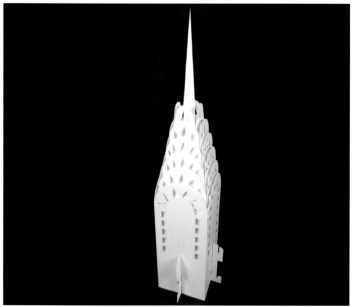

87. It should look like this after step 86 done.

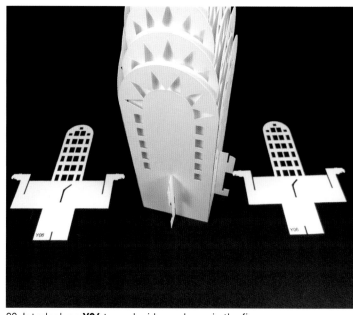

88. Interlock an **Y06** to each side as shown in the figure.

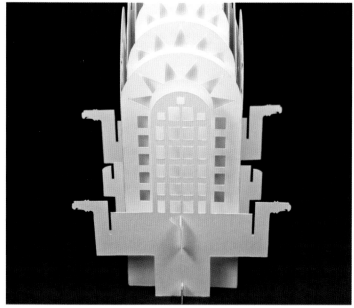

89. It should look like this after step 88 done. Interlock a **X06** to each side as shown in the figure.

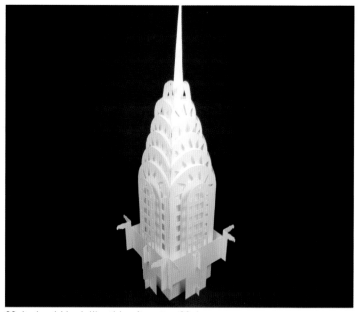

90. It should look like this after step 89 done.

91. Join it to the component shown in step 56 as shown in the figure.

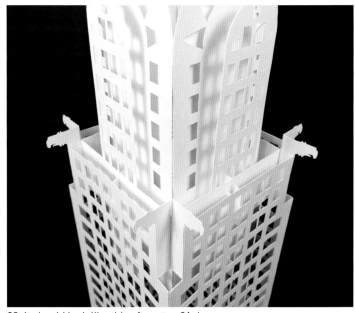

92. It should look like this after step 91 done.

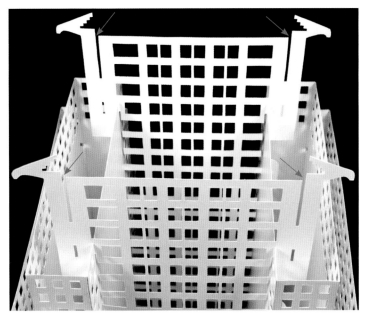

93. It is the component shown in step 49. Interlock the component in step 92 as shown in the figure.

94. It should look like this after step 93 done.

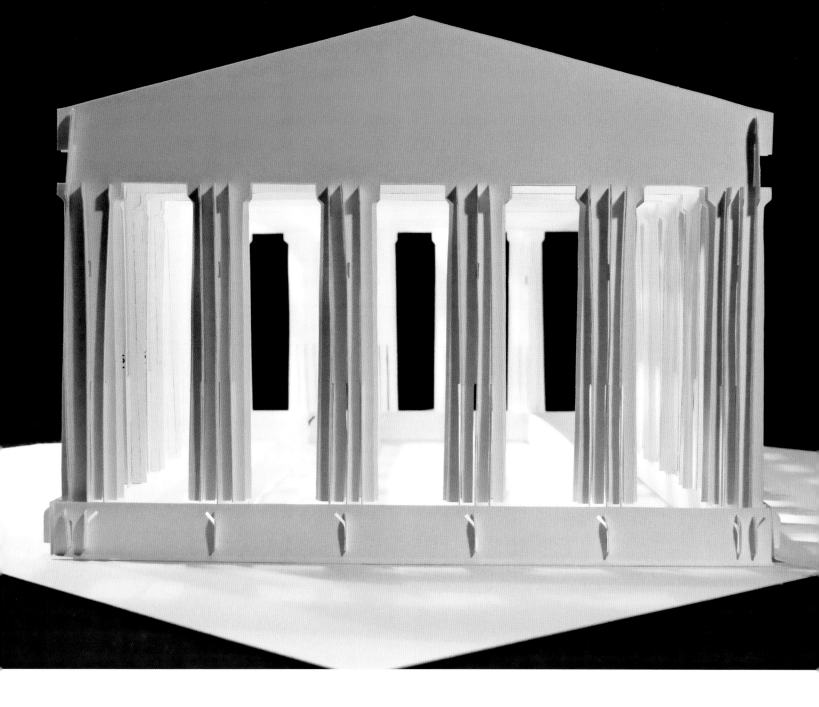

THE PARTHENON
Athens, Greece

The Parthenon was built to give thanks to Athena, the city's patron goddess, for the salvation of Athens and Greece during the Persian Wars. The building was officially called the Temple of Athena the Virgin; "Parthenon" comes from the Greek word parthenos, "virgin." Construction began in 447 BC and the building was substantially completed by 438 BC. It was built under the general supervision of the sculptor Phidias, who also had charge of the sculptural decoration. The architects were Iktinos and Kallikrates. The purpose of the building was to house a 40-foot-high statue of Athena Parthenos sculpted by Pheidias.

The Athens Parthenon is a temple located on the Acropolis, a hill overlooking the city of Athens, Greece. Possible dimensions of the Athens Parthenon: 228 feet or 69.5 meters in length / 111 feet or 34 meters in width / 45 feet or 13.7 meters in height.

Dimensions of the finished model:
(excluding the baseboard)
10.45 inches or 26.5 cm in length
6.15 inches or 15.6 cm in width
4.35 inches or 11 cm in height.

Pieces count: 105 pieces (excluding the baseboard)

Difficulty level: 9/10 (for expert)

Interlock pieces: Assemble the building without glue (excluding the baseboard)

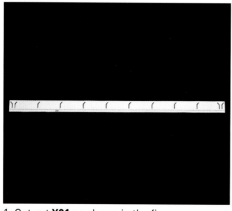

1. Cut out **X01** as shown in the figure.

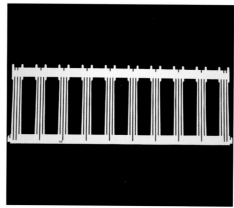

2. Cut out **X02** as shown in the figure. (2 pieces)

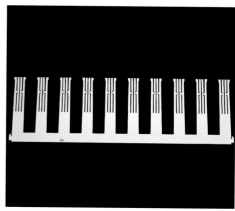

3. Cut out **X03** as shown in the figure. (2 pieces)

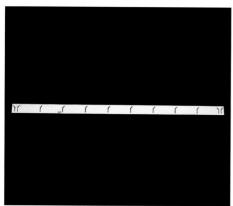

4. Cut out **X04** as shown in the figure. (4 pieces)

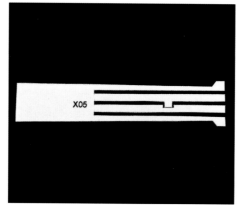

5. Cut out **X05** as shown in the figure. (36 pieces)

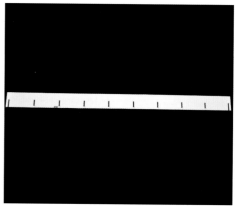

6. Cut out **X06** as shown in the figure.

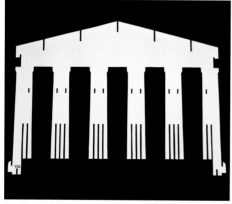

7. Cut out **X07** as shown in the figure.

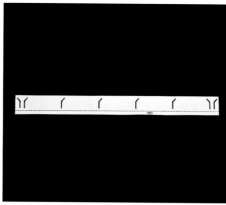

8. Cut out **Y01** as shown in the figure.

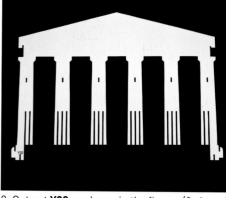

9. Cut out **Y02** as shown in the figure. (2 pieces)

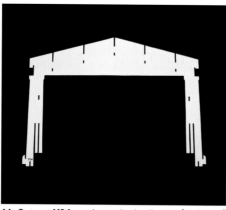

10. Cut out **Y03** as shown in the figure. (2 pieces)

11. Cut out **Y04** as shown in the figure. (8 pieces)

12. Cut out **Y05** as shown in the figure.

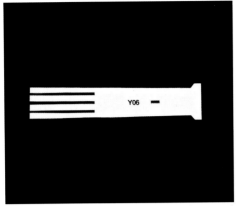

13. Cut out **Y06** as shown in the figure. (8 pieces)

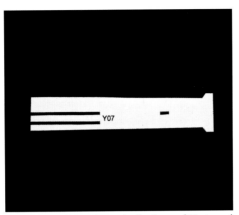

14. Cut out **Y07** as shown in the figure. (36 pieces)

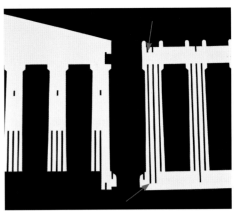

15. Interlock **Y02** to **X02** as shown in the figure.

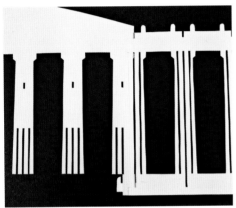

16. It should look like this after **Y02** and **X02** interlocked.

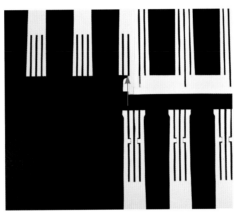

17. Interlock **X03** to **Y02** as shown in the figure.

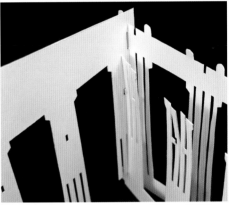

18. It should look like this after **Y02** and **X03** interlocked.

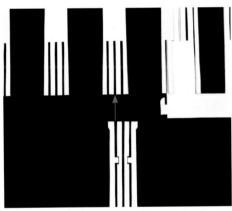

19. Interlock **X04** to **Y02** as shown in the figure.

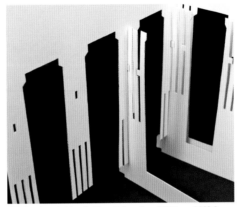

20. It should look like this after **Y02** and **X04** interlocked

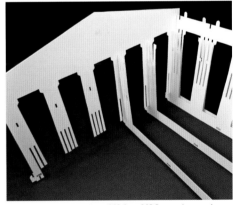

21. Interlock another **X04** to **Y02** as shown in the figure.

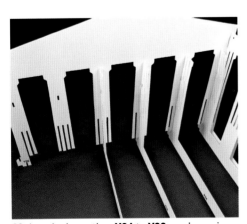

22. Interlock another **X04** to **Y02** as shown in the figure.

23. Interlock another **X04** to **Y02** as shown in the figure.

24. Interlock **X03** to **Y02** as shown in the figure.

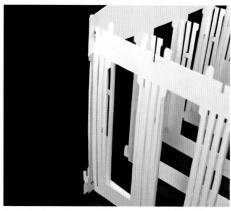

25. Interlock **X02** to **Y02** as shown in the figure.

26. It should look like this after step 25 done. Interlock **Y03** into the slots as shown in the figure.

27. It should look like this after step 26 done. Interlock **Y04** into the slots as shown in the figure.

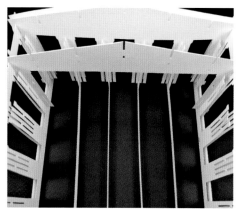

28. It should look like this after step 27 done. Interlock another **Y04** into the slots as shown in the figure.

29. It should look like this after step 28 done. Interlock another **Y04** into the slots as shown in the figure.

30. It should look like this after step 29 done. Interlock another **Y04** into the slots as shown in the figure.

31. It should look like this after step 30 done. Interlock another **Y04** into the slots as shown in the figure.

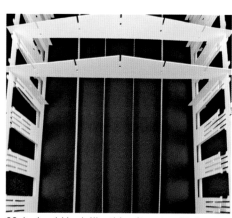

32. It should look like this after step 31 done. Interlock another **Y04** into the slots as shown in the figure.

33. It should look like this after step 32 done. Interlock another **Y04** into the slots as shown in the figure.

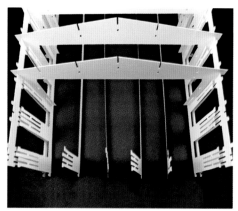

34. It should look like this after step 33 done. Interlock another **Y04** into the slots as shown in the figure.

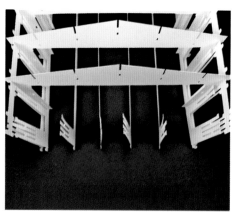

35. It should look like this after step 34 done. Interlock **Y03** into the slots as shown in the figure.

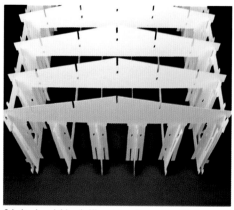

36. It should look like this after step 35 done. Interlock **Y02** into the slots as shown in the figure.

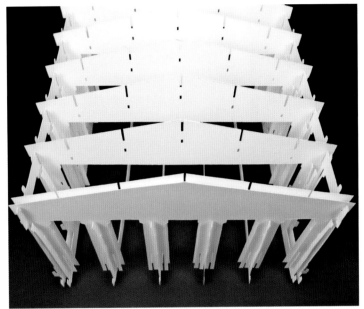

37. It should look like this after step 36 done. Fold **Y01**. Interlock **Y01** into the slots as shown in the figure.

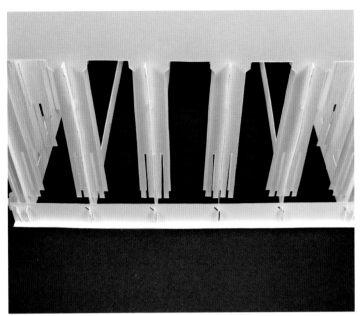

38. It should look like this after step 37 done.

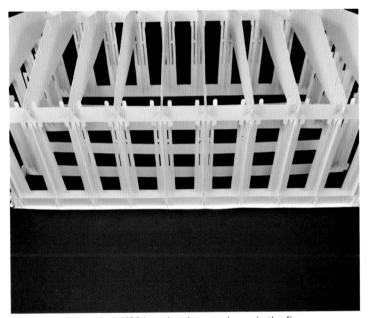

39. Fold **X01**. Interlock **X01** into the slots as shown in the figure.

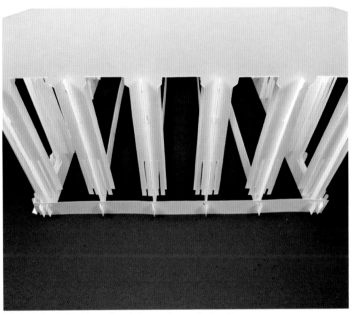

40. Interlock **Y05** into the slots as shown in the figure.

41. Interlock **X07** into the slots as shown in the figure.

42. Slide 10 pieces of **X05** from bottom to Interlock into the slots as shown in the figure.

43. It should look like this after step 42 done.

44. On the opposite side, slide 10 pieces of **X05** from bottom to Interlock into the slots as shown in the figure.

45. Slide 8 pieces of **X05** from bottom to Interlock into the slots as shown in the figure.

46. On the other side, slide 8 pieces of **X05** from bottom to Interlock into the slots as shown in the figure.

47. Tuck 18 pieces of **Y07** to Interlock into the slots as shown in the figure.

48. It should look like this after step 42 done.

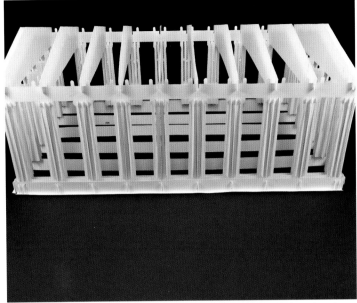

49. On the opposite side, tuck 18 pieces of **Y07** to Interlock into the slots as shown in the figure.

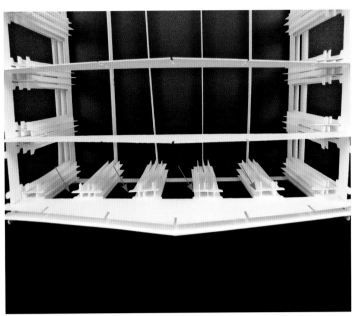

50. Interlock four pieces of **Y06** into the slots as shown in the figure.

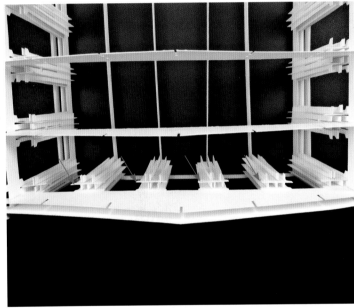

51. On the other side, interlock four pieces of **Y06** into the slots as shown in the figure.

52. Interlock five pieces of **X04** into the slots as shown in the figure.

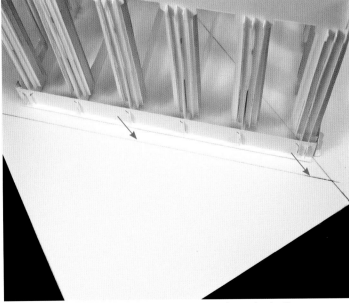

53. Glue folded parts of **Y01** along the line as shown in the figure.

54. It should look like this after **Y01** glued. Erase remaining penciled line.

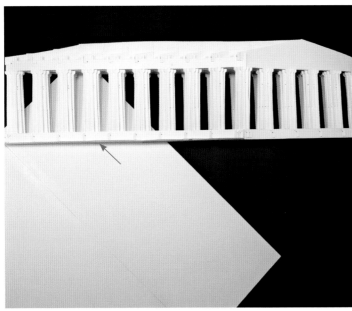

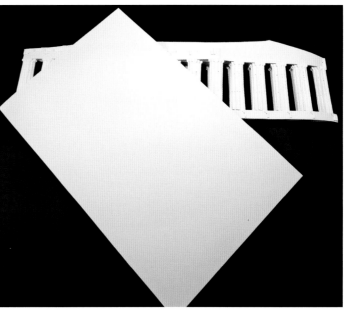

55. Fold down completely the building and apply glue on folded parts of **X01** as shown in the figure.

56. Close the baseboard tightly. The **X01** will find a perfect position to be glued.

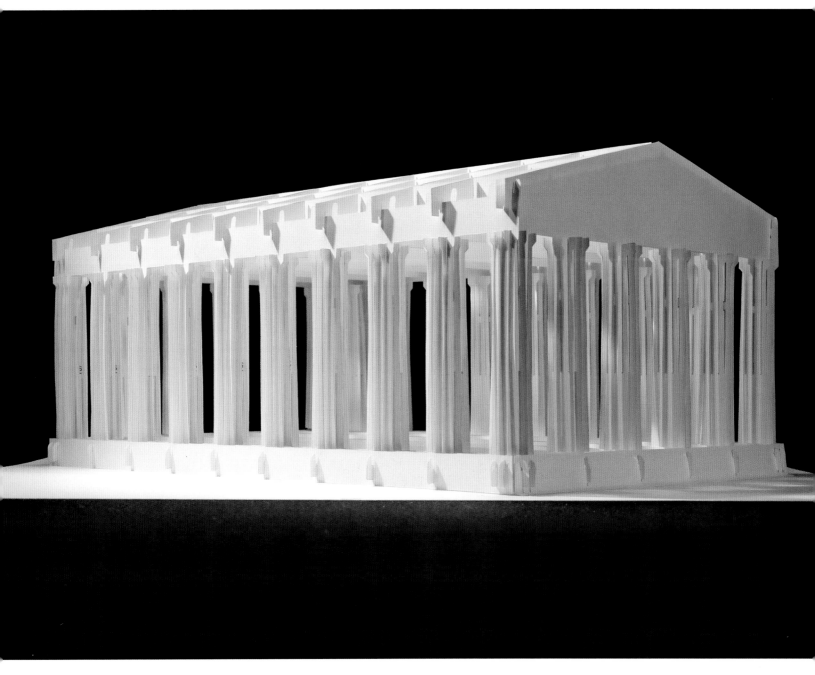

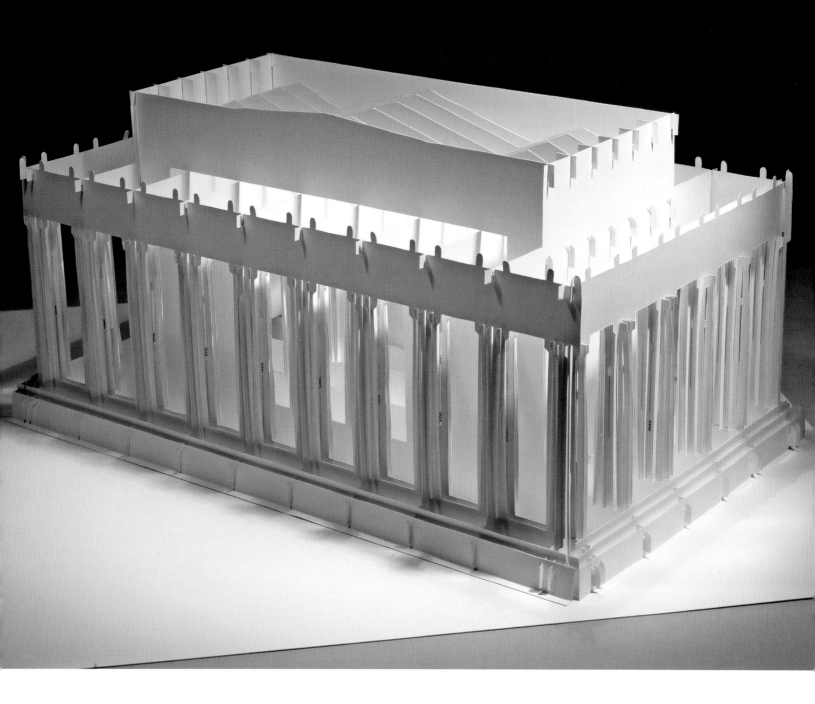

THE LINCOLN MEMORIAL
Washington D.C., USA

The Lincoln Memorial commemorates the life of Abraham Lincoln, the 16th President of the United States. It is located in Potomac Park, Washington, D.C. The construction of the Lincoln Memorial began in 1914; it was dedicated on May 30, 1922. It was designed by Henry Bacon; the style is that of a Greek Doric temple. Inside the building is a huge statue of a sitting Lincoln. It was sculpted by Daniel Chester French, plaster casts of Lincoln's hands and face were used to make the statue. The statue is over three times actual size. On August 28, 1963, Martin Luther King, Jr., made his "I Have a Dream" speech on the steps of the Lincoln Memorial. There is now an inscription on the step where Dr. King stood.

The Lincoln Memorial is located in Potomac Park, Washington, the District. In terms of height, it stands tall at 99 feet or 30 meters. Its depth is measured at 118.5 feet or 36 meters, while its width is 189.7 feet or 57.8 meters.

Dimensions of the finished model:
(excluding the baseboard)
10.49 inches or 26.6 cm in length
6.34 inches or 16.1 cm in width
4.97 inches or 12.6 cm in height.

Pieces count: 138 pieces (excluding the baseboard)

Difficulty level: 9/10 (for expert)

Interlock pieces: Assemble the building without glue (excluding the baseboard).

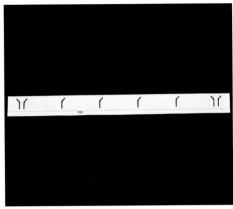

1. Cut out **Y01** as shown in the figure.

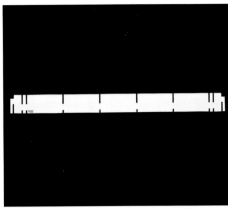

2. Cut out **Y02** as shown in the figure. (2 pieces)

3. Cut out **Y03** as shown in the figure. (2 pieces)

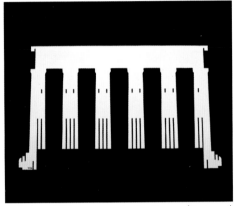

4. Cut out **Y04** as shown in the figure. (2 pieces)

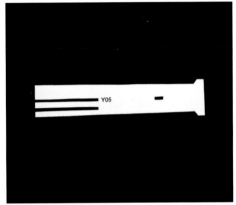

5. Cut out **Y05** as shown in the figure. (36 pieces)

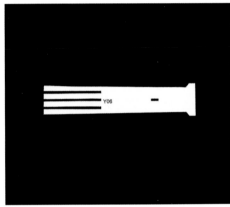

6. Cut out **Y06** as shown in the figure. (20 pieces)

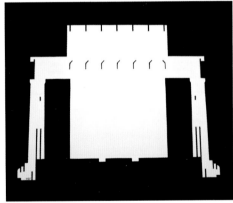

7. Cut out **Y07** as shown in the figure. (2 pieces)

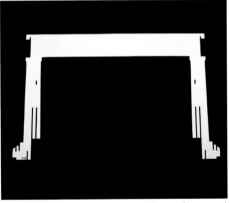

8. Cut out **Y08** as shown in the figure. (2 pieces)

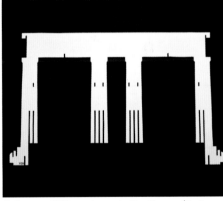

9. Cut out **Y09** as shown in the figure. (2 pieces)

10. Cut out **Y10** as shown in the figure. (2 pieces)

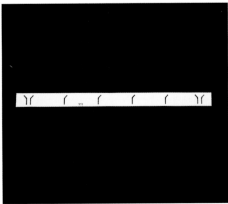

11. Cut out **Y11** as shown in the figure.

12. Cut out **X01** as shown in the figure.

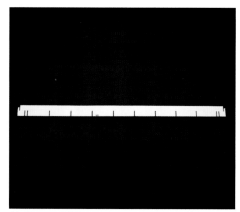

13. Cut out **X02** as shown in the figure. (2 pieces)

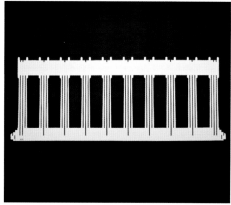

14. Cut out **X03** as shown in the figure. (2 pieces)

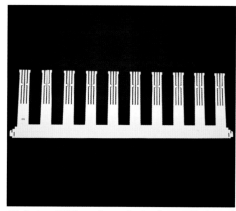

15. Cut out **X04** as shown in the figure. (2 pieces)

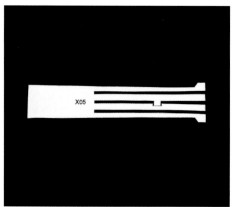

16. Cut out **X05** as shown in the figure. (46 pieces)

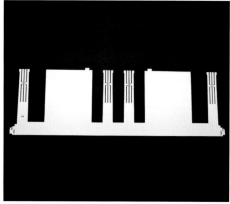

17. Cut out **X06** as shown in the figure.

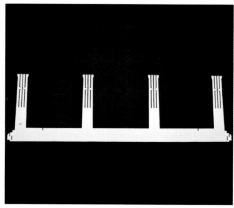

18. Cut out **X07** as shown in the figure. (2 pieces)

19. Cut out **X08** as shown in the figure.

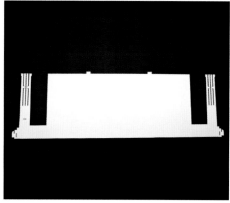

20. Cut out **X09** as shown in the figure.

21. Cut out **X10** as shown in the figure.

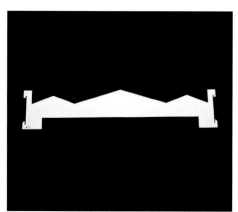

22. Cut out **X11** as shown in the figure. (5 pieces)

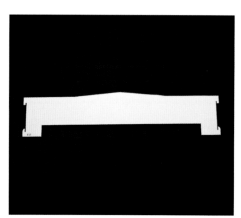

23. Cut out **X12** as shown in the figure.

24. Cut out **X13** as shown in the figure.

25. Interlock **X03** to **Y03** as shown in the figure.

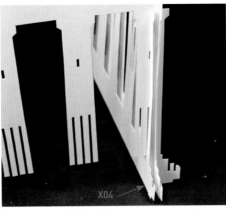

26. Interlock **X04** to **Y03** as shown in the figure.

27. Interlock **X06** to **Y03** as shown in the figure.

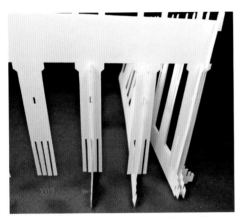

28. Interlock **X07** to **Y03** as shown in the figure.

29. Interlock another **X07** to **Y03** as shown in the figure.

30. Interlock **X08** to **Y03** as shown in the figure.

31. Interlock **X09** to **Y03** as shown in the figure.

32. Interlock **X04** to **Y03** as shown in the figure.

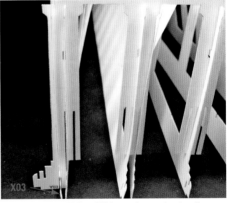

33. Interlock **X03** to **Y03** as shown in the figure.

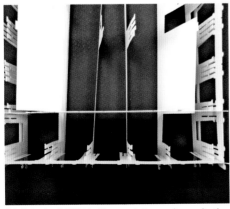

34. Interlock **Y07** to these slots as shown in the figure.

35. Interlock **Y08** to these slots as shown in the figure.

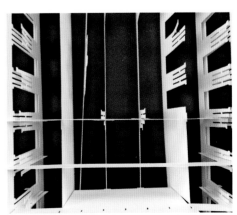

36. Interlock **Y09** to these slots as shown in the figure.(

37. Interlock **Y10** to these slots as shown in the figure.

38. Interlock **Y10** to these slots as shown in the figure.

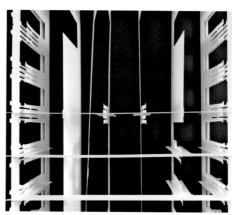

39. Interlock **Y09** to these slots as shown in the figure.

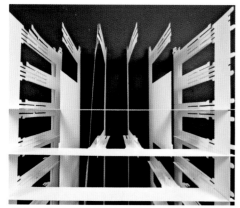

40. Interlock **Y08** to these slots as shown in the figure.

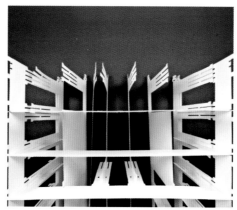

41. Interlock **Y07** to these slots as shown in the figure.

42. Interlock **Y04** to these slots as shown in the figure.

43. Interlock **Y03** to these slots as shown in the figure.

44. In opposite side, interlock another **Y04** to these slots as shown in the figure.

45. Slide **X05** from bottom to Interlock into the slot as shown in the figure.

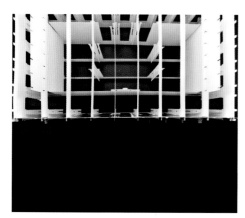

46. Interlock 10 pieces of **X05** total as shown in the figure.

47. It should look like this after step 46 done.

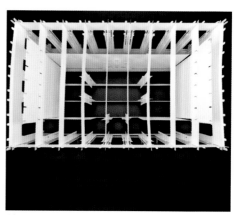

48. Rotate the building 180 degrees. Interlock 10 pieces of **X05** total as shown in the figure.

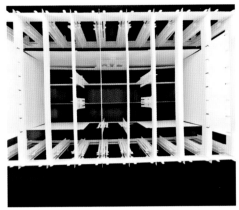

49. It should look like this after step 48 done.

50. Slide 12 pieces of **X05** total from bottom to Interlock into the slots as shown in the figure.

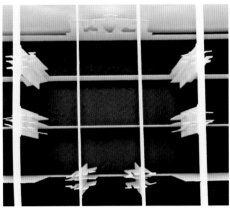

51. It should look like this after step 50 done.

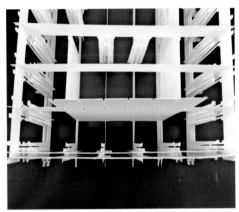

52. Slide 7 pieces of **X05** total from bottom to Interlock into the slots as shown in the figure.

53. It should look like this after step 52 done.

54. Rotate the building 180 degrees. Slide 7 pieces of **X05** total from bottom to Interlock into the slots as shown in the figure.

55. It should look like this after step 54 done.

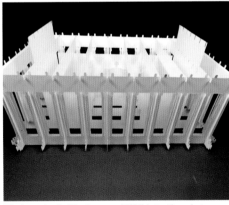

56. Interlock 18 pieces of **Y05** into the slots as shown in the figure.

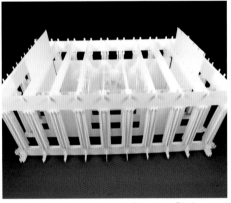

57. It should look like this after step 56 done.

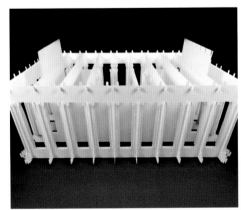

58. Rotate the building 180 degrees. Interlock 18 pieces of **Y05** into the slots as shown in the figure.

59. It should look like this after step 58 done.

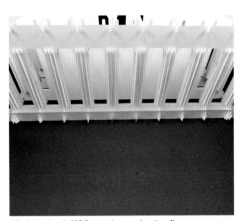

60. Interlock **X02** as shown in the figure.

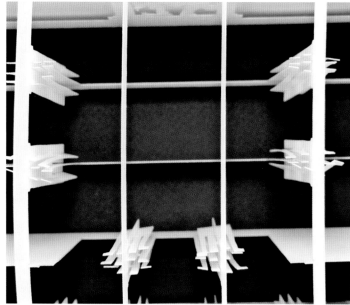

61. Interlock 12 pieces of **Y06** into the slots as shown in the figure.

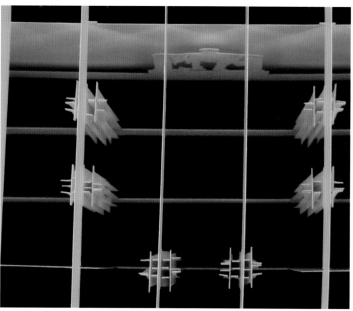

62. It should look like this after step 61 done.

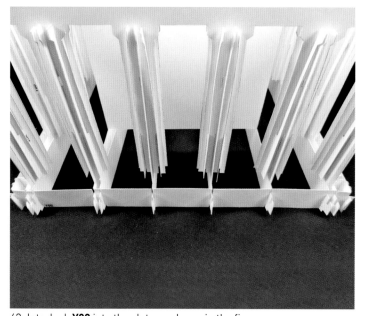

63. Interlock **Y02** into the slots as shown in the figure.

64. Rotate the building 180 degrees. Interlock another **Y02**.as shown in the figure.

65. Interlock **X10** into the slots as shown in the figure.

66. Interlock **X11** into the slots as shown in the figure.

67. Interlock another **X11** into the slots as shown in the figure.

68. Interlock another **X11** into the slots as shown in the figure.

69. Interlock another **X11** into the slots as shown in the figure.

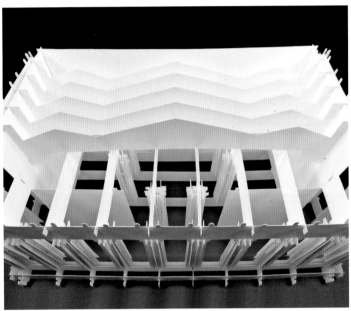

70. Interlock another **X11** into the slots as shown in the figure.

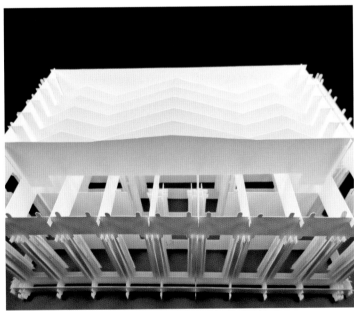

71. Interlock another **X11** into the slots as shown in the figure.

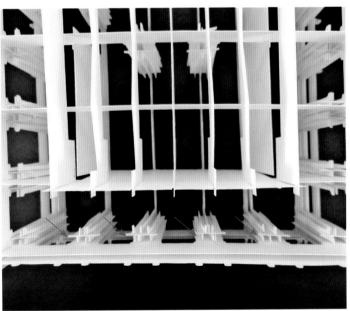

72. Interlock four pieces of **Y06** into the slots as shown in the figure.

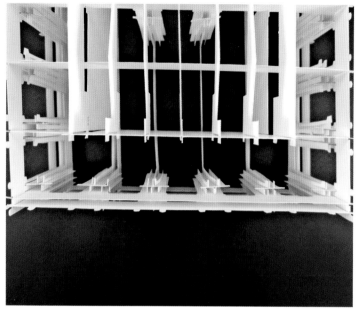

73. Rotate the building 180 degrees. Interlock four pieces of **Y06** into the slots as shown in the figure.

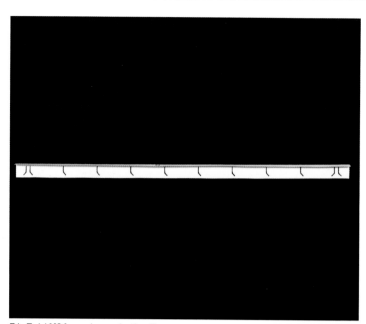

74. Fold **X01** as shown in the figure.

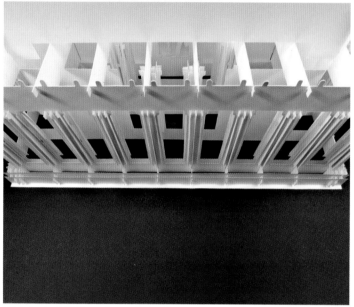

75. Interlock **X01** as shown in the figure.

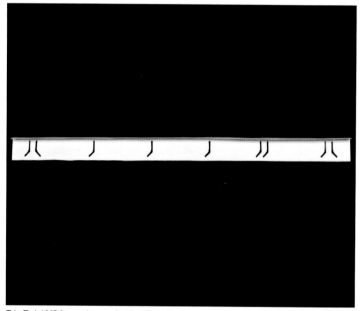

76. Fold **Y01** as shown in the figure.

77. Interlock **Y01** as shown in the figure.

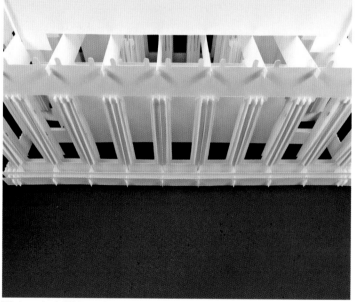

78. Interlock **X13** as shown in the figure.

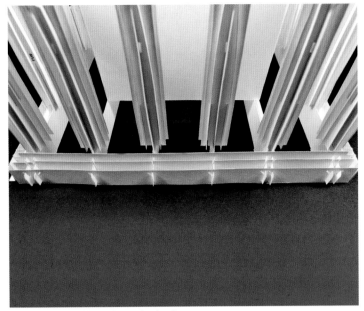

79. Interlock **Y11** as shown in the figure.

80. Glue **X01** and **Y01** onto the baseboard as shown in the figure.

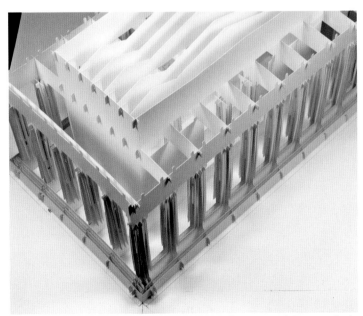

81. It should look like this after step 80 done. Erase remaining penciled lines.

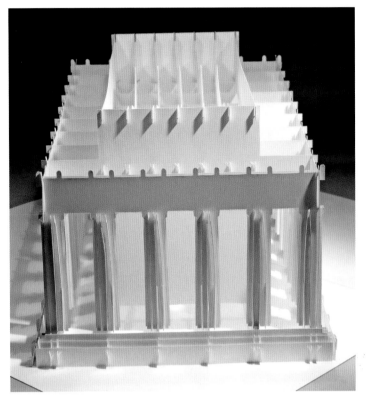

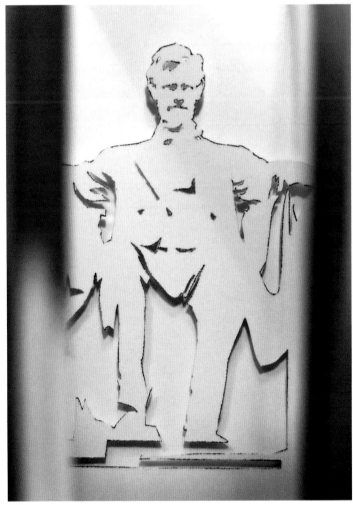

THE WESTMINSTER PALACE
London, England

The Palace of Westminster was built for Edward the Confessor in the 11th century as a London home for him. During the Reign of Henry VIII in 1512 a large part of the Palace burnt down and this was when its role as a Royal residence ended. On 16 October 1834 another and even more devastating fire virtually destroyed the Houses of Parliament, the only structures to survive were Westminster Hall, Chapter House of St. Stephens, the Chapel of St. Mary Undercroft, the cloisters and the Jewel tower. After the fire of 1834, the reconstruction of the Houses of Parliament contract was won by architect Charles Berry, who would be assisted by Augustus Pugin, who built it in the Gothic Revival Style. The construction began in 1837 and was not completely finished until 1870s. Both men failed to live long enough to see the project completed. It was the target of the now famous Gunpowder Plot which is commemorated on November 5th as Guy Fawkes Day.

The Palace of Westminster is located in the heart of the London borough of the City of Westminster, England.

Dimensions of the finished model:
(excluding the baseboard)
25.78 inches or 65.5 cm in length
11.64 inches or 29.6 cm in width
10.28 inches or 26.1 cm in height.

Pieces count: 71 pieces (exclude baseboard)

Difficulty level: 10/10 (for expert)

Interlock pieces: Assemble the building without glue (excluding the baseboard).

1. Cut out **Y01** as shown in the figure.

2. Cut out **Y02** as shown in the figure. (2 pieces)

3. Cut out **Y03** as shown in the figure.

4. Cut out **Y04** as shown in the figure.

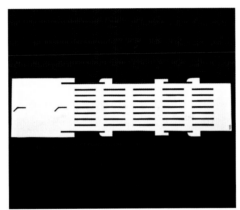

5. Cut out **Y05** as shown in the figure.

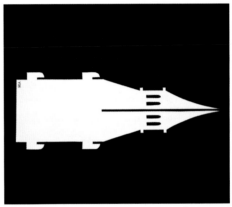

6. Cut out **Y06** as shown in the figure. (2 pieces)

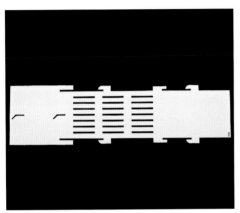

7. Cut out **Y07** as shown in the figure. (2 pieces)

8. Cut out **Y08** as shown in the figure.

9. Cut out **Y09** as shown in the figure.

10. Cut out **Y10** as shown in the figure. (2 pieces)

11. Cut out **Y10b** as shown in the figure. (2 pieces)

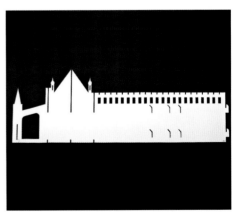

12. Cut out **Y11** as shown in the figure.

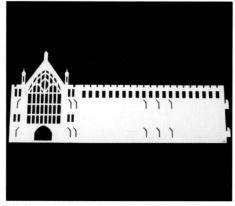

13. Cut out **Y12** as shown in the figure.

14. Cut out **Y13** as shown in the figure.

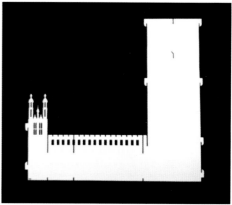

15. Cut out **Y14** as shown in the figure. (2 pieces)

16. Cut out **Y15** as shown in the figure.

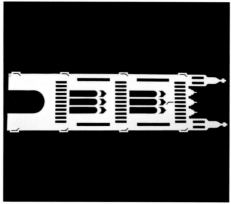

17. Cut out **Y16** as shown in the figure.

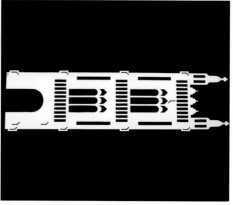

18. Cut out **Y17** as shown in the figure.

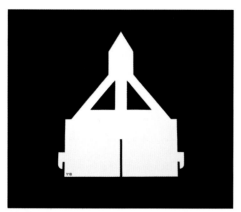

19. Cut out **Y18** as shown in the figure.

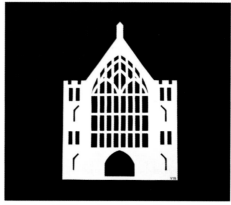

20. Cut out **Y19** as shown in the figure.

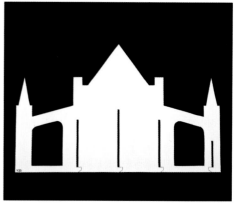

21. Cut out **Y20** as shown in the figure. (3 pieces)

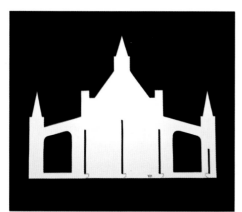

22. Cut out **Y21** as shown in the figure.

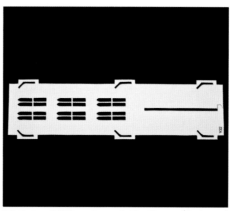

23. Cut out **Y22** as shown in the figure. (2 pieces)

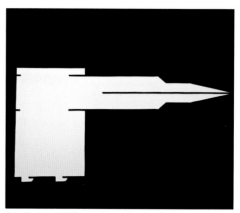

24. Cut out **Y23** as shown in the figure.

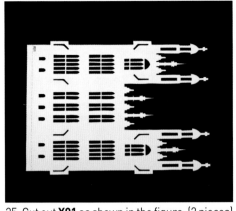

25. Cut out **X01** as shown in the figure. (2 pieces)

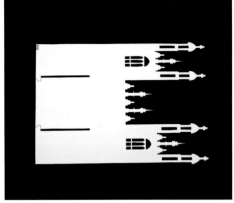

26. Cut out **X02** as shown in the figure. (2 pieces)

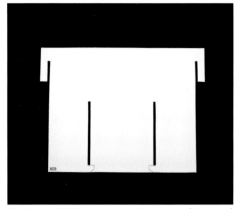

27. Cut out **X03** as shown in the figure. (2 pieces)

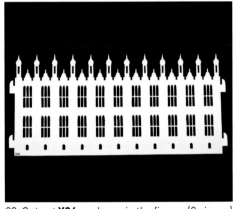

28. Cut out **X04** as shown in the figure. (2 pieces)

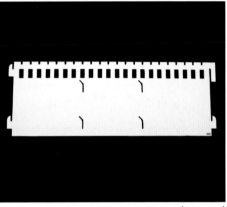

29. Cut out **X05** as shown in the figure. (2 pieces)

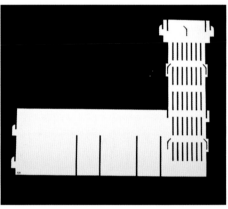

30. Cut out **X06** as shown in the figure.

31. Cut out **X07** as shown in the figure.

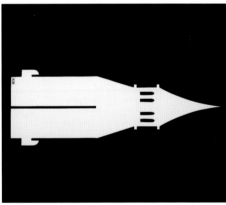

32. Cut out **X08** as shown in the figure.

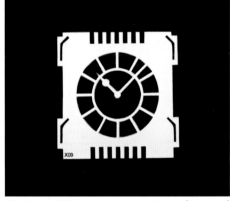

33. Cut out **X09** as shown in the figure. (2 pieces)

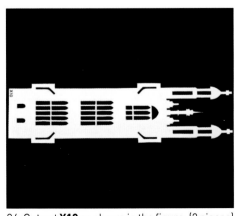

34. Cut out **X10** as shown in the figure. (2 pieces)

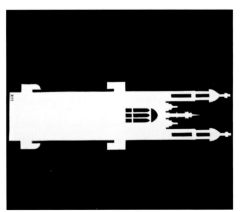

35. Cut out **X11** as shown in the figure. (2 pieces)

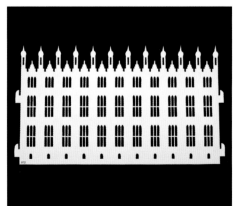

36. Cut out **X12** as shown in the figure

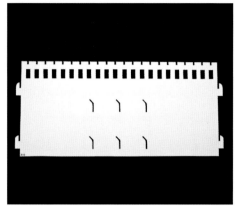

37. Cut out **X13** as shown in the figure.

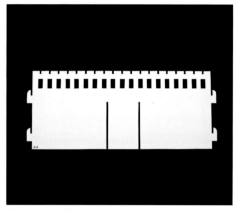

38. Cut out **X14** as shown in the figure.

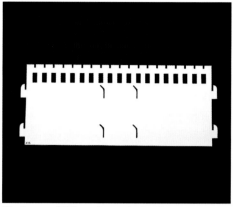

39. Cut out **X15** as shown in the figure.

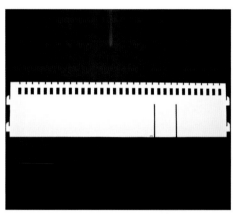

40. Cut out **X16** as shown in the figure.

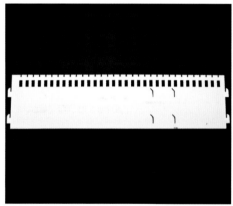

41. Cut out **X16b** as shown in the figure.

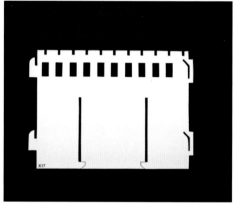

42. Cut out **X17** as shown in the figure.

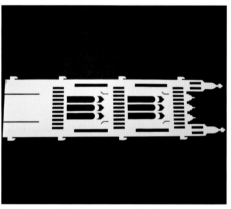

43. Cut out **X18** as shown in the figure.

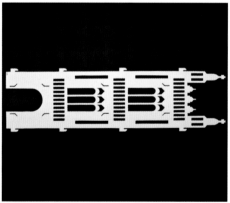

44. Cut out **X19** as shown in the figure.

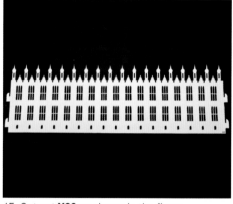

45. Cut out **X20** as shown in the figure.

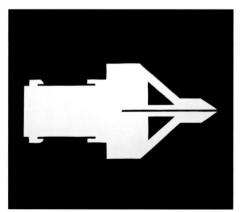

46. Cut out **X21** as shown in the figure.

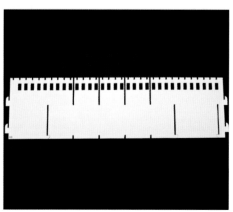

47. Cut out **X22** as shown in the figure.

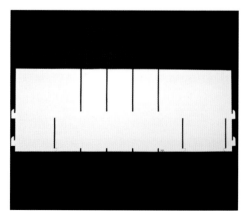

48. Cut out **X23** as shown in the figure.

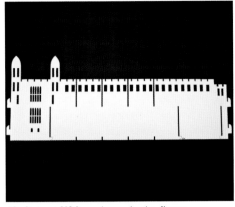

49. Cut out **X24** as shown in the figure.

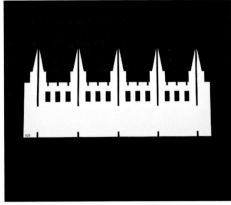

50. Cut out **X25** as shown in the figure.

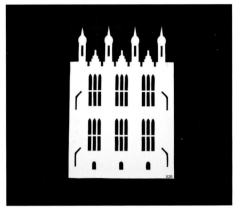

51. Cut out **X26** as shown in the figure.

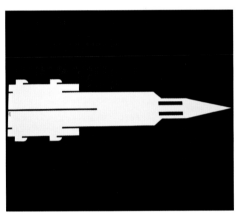

52. Cut out **X27** as shown in the figure.

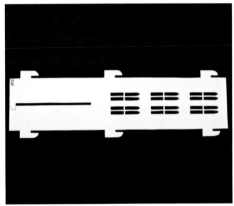

53. Cut out **X28** as shown in the figure. (2 pieces)

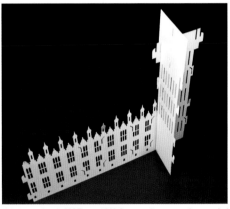

54. Interlock **X07** and **Y04** together as shown in the figure.

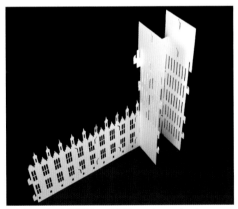

55. Interlock **Y05** into **X07** as shown in the figure.

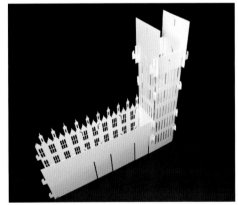

56. Interlock **X06** into the slots as shown in the figure.

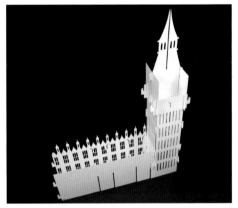

57. Interlock **Y06** into the slots as shown in the figure.

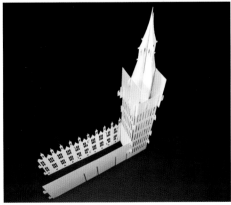

58. Interlock **X08** into the slots as shown in the figure.

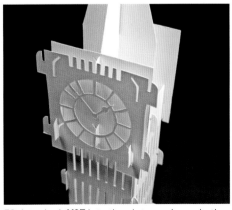

59. Interlock **Y07** into the slots as shown in the figure.

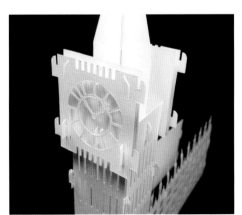

60. Interlock another **Y07** into the slots as shown in the figure.

61. Interlock **X09** into the slots as shown in the figure.

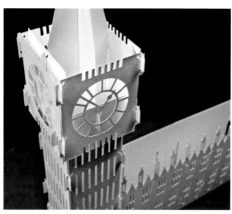

62. Interlock another **X09** into the slots as shown in the figure.

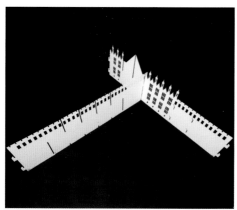

63. Interlock **Y08** and **X22** together as shown in the figure.

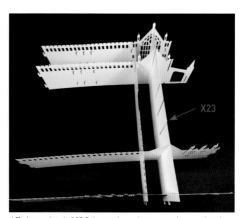

64. Interlock **Y09** and **X22** together as shown in the figure.

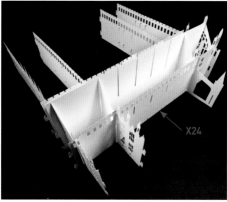

65. Interlock **Y11** and **X22** together as shown in the figure.

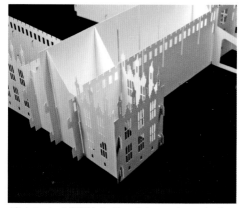

66. Interlock **Y12** and **X22** together as shown in the figure.

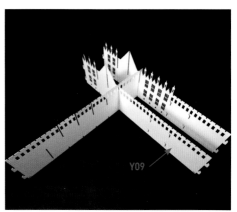

67. Interlock **X23** into the slots as shown in the figure.

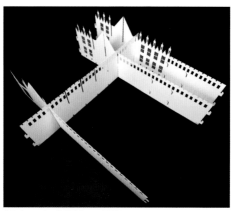

68. Interlock **X24** into the slots as shown in the figure.

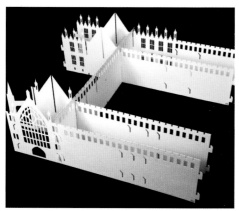

69. Interlock **X26** into the slots as shown in the figure.

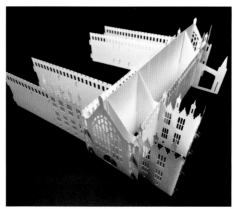

70. Interlock **Y19** into the slots as shown in the figure.(

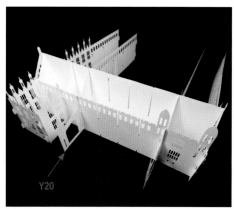

71. Interlock **Y20** into the slots as shown in the figure.

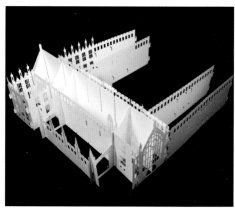

72.Interlock **X25** into the slots as shown in the figure.

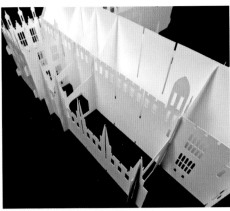

73. Interlock another **Y20** into the slots as shown in the figure.

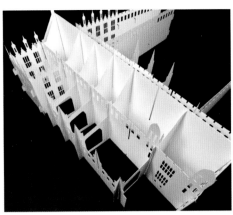

74. Interlock another **Y20** into the slots as shown in the figure.

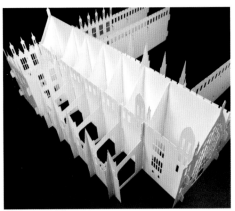

75. Interlock **Y21** into the slots as shown in the figure.

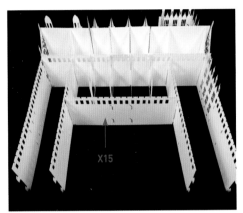

76. Interlock **X15** into the slots as shown in the figure.

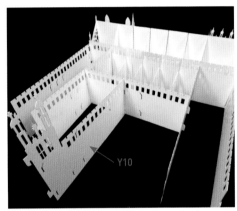

77. Interlock **Y10** into **X15** as shown in the figure.

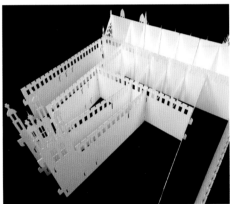

78. Interlock another **Y10** into **X15** as shown in the figure.

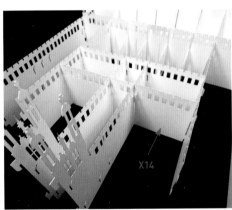

79. Interlock **X14** into the slots as shown in the figure.

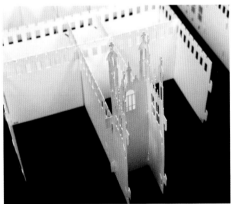

80. Interlock **X11** into the slots as shown in the figure.

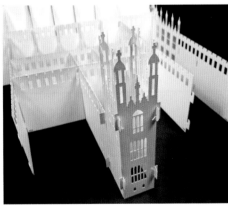

81. Interlock **X10** into the slots as shown in the figure.

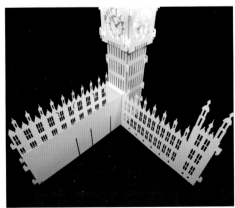

82. Interlock **Y01** into the slots as shown in the figure.

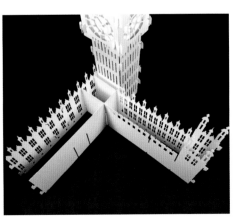

83. Interlock **Y02** into the slots as shown in the figure.

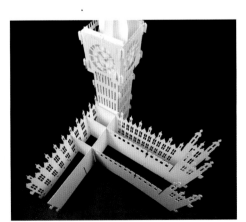

84. Interlock another **Y02** into the slots as shown in the figure.

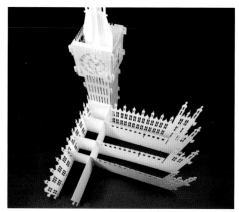

85. Interlock another **Y03** into the slots as shown in the figure.

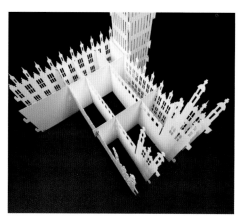

86. Interlock **X03** into the slots as shown in the figure.

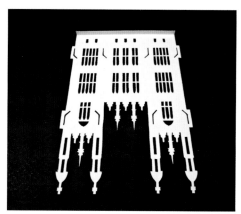

87. Fold the bottom part of **X01** as shown in the figure.

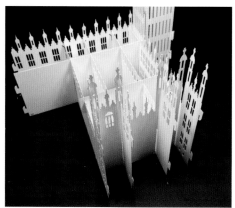

88. Interlock **X02** into the slots as shown in the figure.

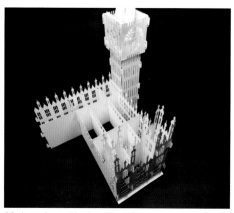

89. Interlock **X01** into the slots as shown in the figure.

90. Take the component from step 81. Interlock two components together as shown in the figure.

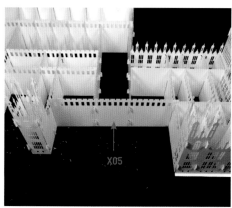

91. Interlock **X05** into the slots as shown in the figure.

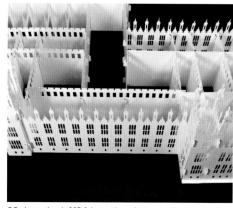

92. Interlock **X04** into the slots as shown in the figure.

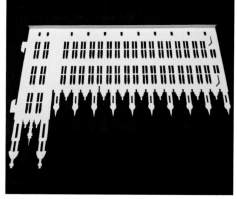

93. Fold the bottom part of **Y13** as shown in the figure.

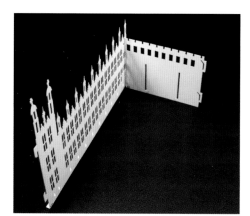

94. Interlock **Y13** and **X17** together as shown in the figure.

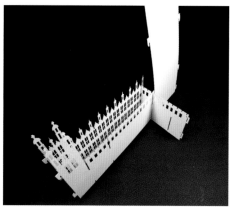

95. Interlock **Y14** and **X17** together as shown in the figure.

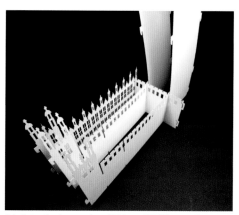

96. Interlock another **Y14** and **X17** together as shown in the figure.

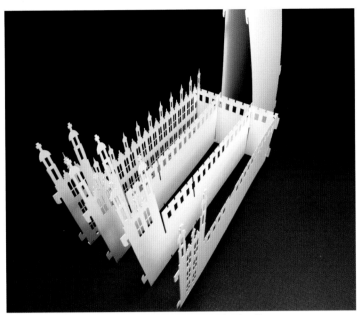

97. Interlock **Y15** and **X17** together as shown in the figure.

98. Interlock **X03** into the slots as shown in the figure.

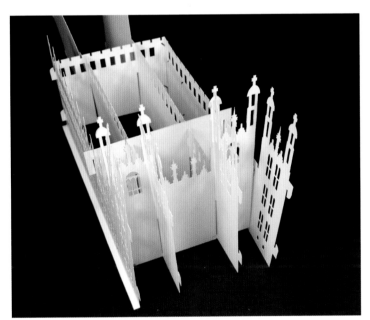

99. Interlock **X02** into the slots as shown in the figure.

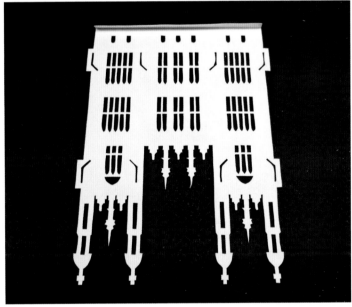

100. Fold the bottom part of **X01** as shown in the figure.

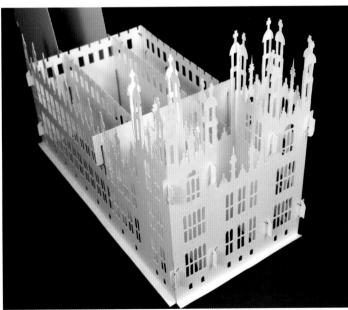

101. Interlock **X01** into the slots as shown in the figure.

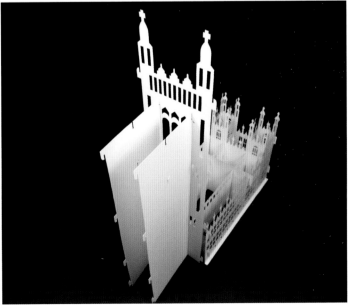

102. Interlock **X18** into the slots as shown in the figure.

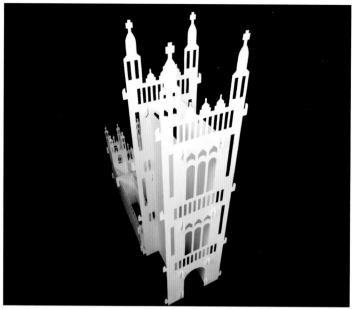

103. Interlock **X19** into the slots as shown in the figure.

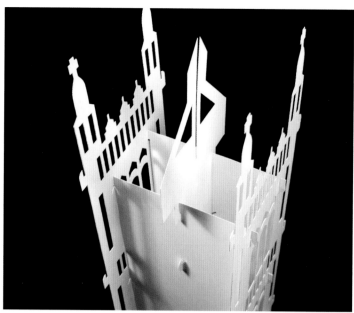

104. Interlock **X21** into the slots as shown in the figure.

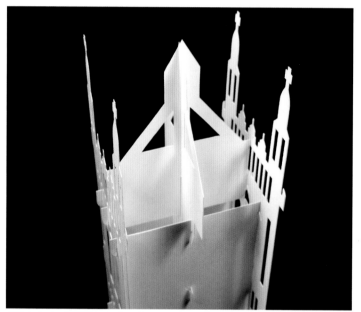

105. Interlock **Y18** into the slots as shown in the figure.

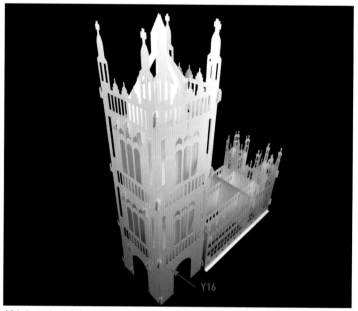

106. Interlock **Y16** into the slots as shown in the figure.

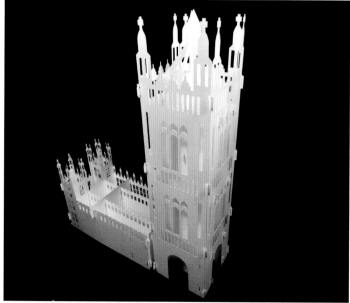

107. Interlock **Y17** into the slots as shown in the figure.

108. Take the component from step 92. Connect two components with **X16b** as shown in the figure.

109. Interlock **X20** into the slots as shown in the figure.

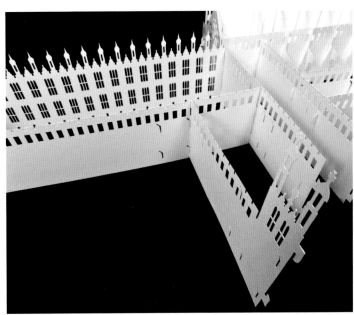

110. Interlock **Y10b** into **X16b** as shown in the figure.

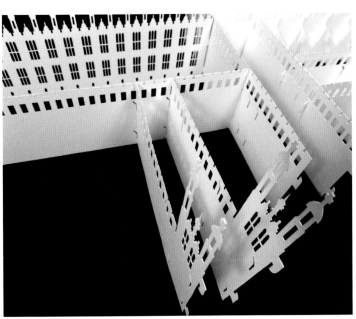

111. Interlock another **Y10b** into **X16b** as shown in the figure.

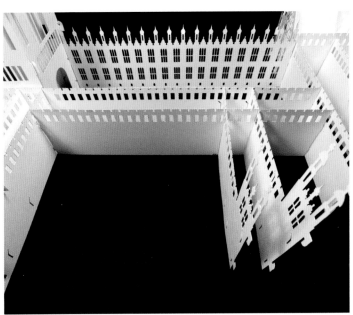

112. Interlock **X16** into the slots as shown in the figure.

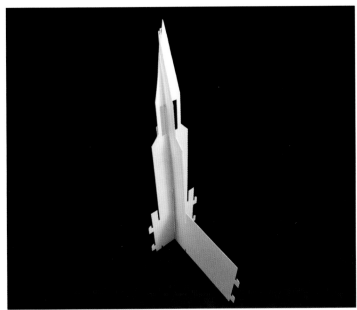

113. Interlock **Y23** and **X27** together as shown in the figure.

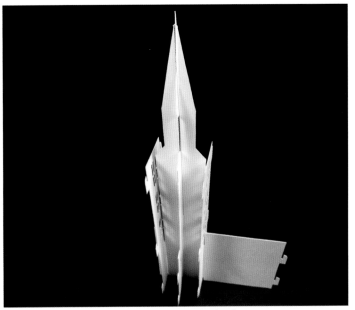

114. Interlock two **X28** into **Y23** as shown in the figure.

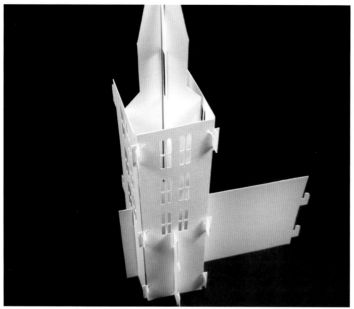

115. Interlock **Y22** into the slots as shown in the figure.

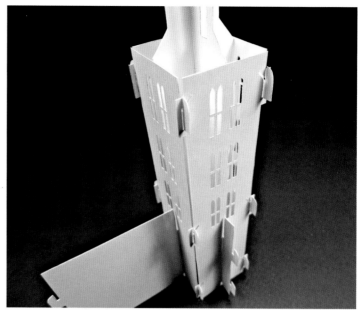

116. Interlock another **Y22** into the slots as shown in the figure.

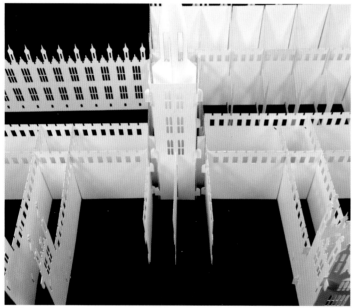

117. Interlock it into **Y11** and **Y12** as shown in the figure.

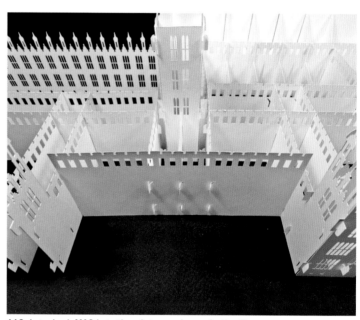

118. Interlock **X13** into the slots as shown in the figure.

119. Interlock **X11** into the slots as shown in the figure.

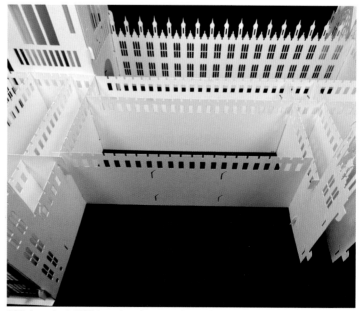

120. Interlock **X05** into the slots as shown in the figure.

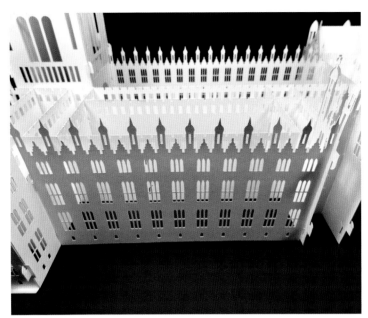

121. Interlock **X04** into the slots as shown in the figure.

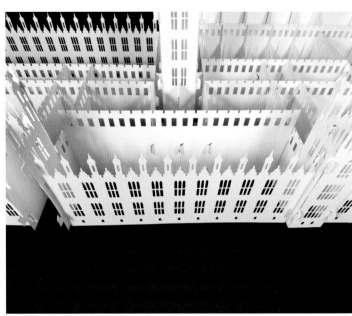

122. Interlock **X12** into the slots as shown in the figure.

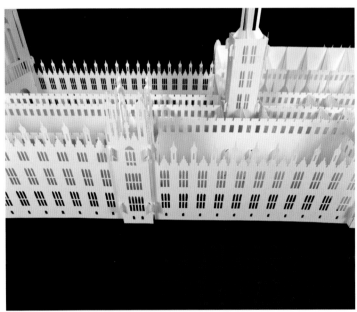

123. Interlock **X10** into the slots as shown in the figure. It is done.

124. Glue **Y13** along the 45 degrees penciled line as shown in the figure. Erase remain penciled lines.

125. Fold down the building completely and apply glue on both **X01**. Close the baseboard tightly. Both **X01** will find the perfect positions to be glued.

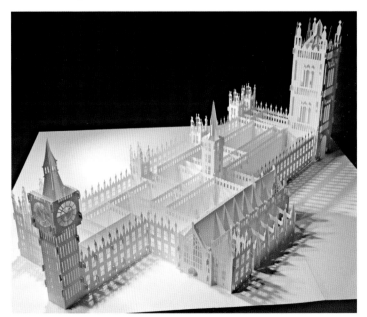

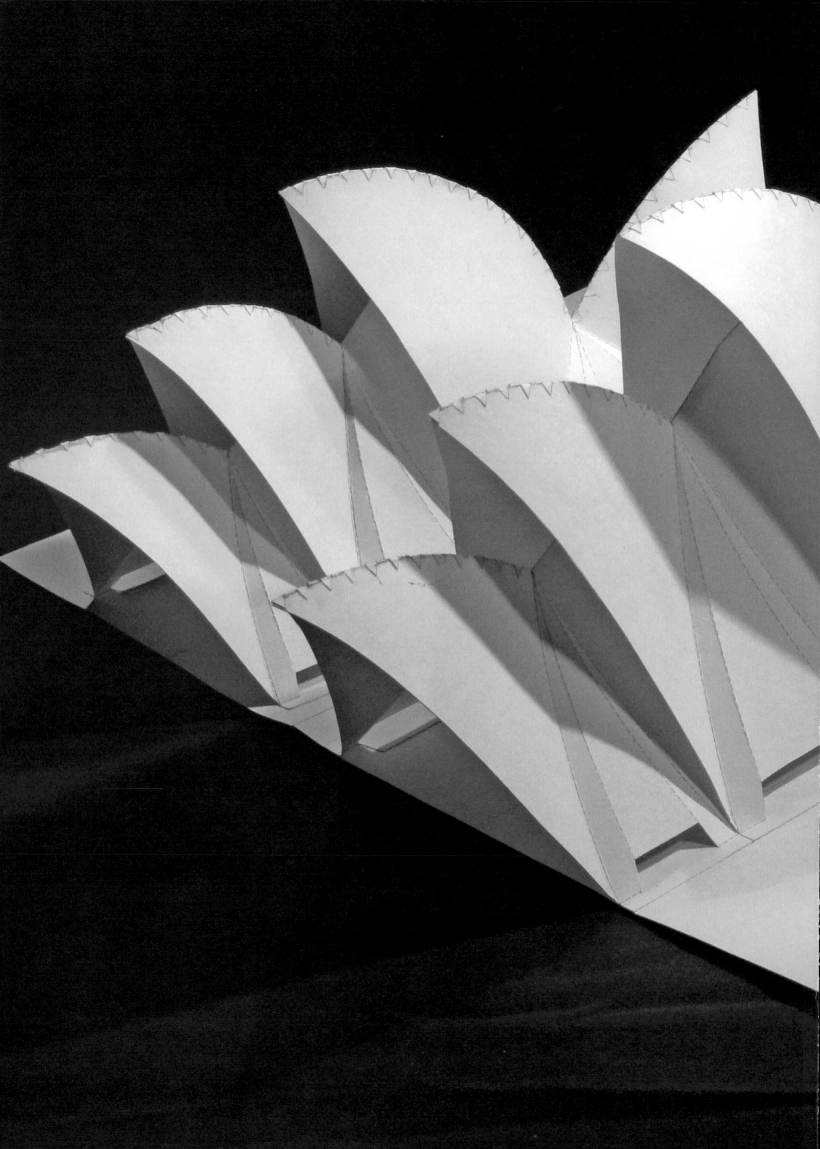